For dearest

Thanks for a
visit to Dun
with much love
Jane, Pete, Euan & Alastair
xxxx

A Generous
Helping

Sept 2011

A Generous Helping

Treasured recipes from the people of Queensland

Madonna King and
Alison Alexander

ABC
Books

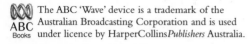 The ABC 'Wave' device is a trademark of the
Australian Broadcasting Corporation and is used
under licence by HarperCollins*Publishers* Australia.

First published in Australia in 2011
by HarperCollins*Publishers* Australia Pty Limited
ABN 36 009 913 517
harpercollins.com.au

Foreword by Madonna King
Introduction by Alison Alexander
Copyright in this collection HarperCollins*Publishers* 2011
Copyright individual recipes resides with the contributors

HarperCollins*Publishers*
Level 13, 201 Elizabeth Street, Sydney NSW 2000, Australia
31 View Road, Glenfield, Auckland 0627, New Zealand
A 53, Sector 57, NOIDA, UP, India
77–85 Fulham Palace Road, London W6 8JB, United Kingdom
2 Bloor Street East, 20th floor, Toronto, Ontario M4W 1A8, Canada
10 East 53rd Street, New York NY 10022, USA

National Library of Australia Cataloguing-in-Publication data:

King, Madonna, 1965–
    A generous helping / Madonna King and Alison Alexander.
    1st ed.
    ISBN: 978 0 7333 3039 1 (pbk.)
    Includes index.
    Cooking, Australian.
    Alexander, Alison, 1949–
641.5

Cover design by Jane Waterhouse, HarperCollins Design Studio
Cover images by shutterstock.com
Typeset in Sabon 10/13.5pt by Letter Spaced
Printed and bound in Australia by Griffin Press
70gsm Classic used by HarperCollins*Publishers* is a natural, recyclable product made from wood grown
in sustainable forests. The manufacturing processes conform to the environmental regulations in the
country of origin, Finland.

5 4 3 2 1   11 12 13 14

CONTENTS

FOREWORD

Not everyone is lucky enough to have a kitchen mum. I did, and each afternoon my four brothers and I would race home from school in Roma ready to feast on what Mum had lovingly prepared that day.

Chocolate cake was a special afternoon tea treat, but so too was her lemon pie, caramel tart and apricot pie. Mum's pavlova, packed with passionfruit and strawberries, was my favourite and the one I chose to include here (page 96). We'd wash down generous helpings with Mum's home-made ginger beer, which was stocked high in the laundry with the stewed pears and apples.

That's just how it was, for as long as I can remember. Mum always seemed disappointed if we didn't ask for a second piece. My brothers even claimed to hide slices of cake and sell them at school. I'm not sure if that was fact or fiction, but I'd caught onto the idea by the time we moved to Dalby and remember regularly swapping Mum's delicacies for money to buy a sausage roll at both St Mary's and Dalby State High School tuckshops.

When I had my own little ones, I sometimes wondered how much they would miss out on without a kitchen mum. At least I did, until I met Alison Alexander, the inspiration and ideas woman behind this book. Alison, like most people in our state, was devastated by the floods that tore at our homes and our hearts early this year. Like so many others, she wanted to do more than clean the homes of friends and colleagues.

She wanted to replace the warmth in their kitchens, the recipes that families had loved and turned to in hard times and during celebrations; food that had been served up when families dealt with tough conversations, and those enjoyed as children around dinner tables enjoyed birthdays, graduations, engagements and the birth of their own children.

During a fortnightly spot on my 612 ABC Brisbane radio program, Alison had taken on the task of teaching me to cook putting up with an endless stream of silly questions. I knew her idea could be a winning ingredient as people rebuilt their lives and made their kitchens home again to soothing soups and playful banter.

A Generous Helping is not my book. Nor is it Alison's. It's *your* book, filled with your recipes, for those who might have lost theirs. It's for the mums and grandmums and dads who like to clear the kitchen bench and create.

Even the name was a difficult decision, because you came up with so many good ideas. From *Meals for the Mud Army* to *Sweet Relief, Mud Cakes, Floody Delicious* and *Recipes for Relief* – we fought over them, leaving the final decision to our guide on this project, Jo Mackay from HarperCollins*Publishers*. But *A Generous Helping* says it all. The food is as generous as the offers of help that flooded in during January. We all wanted to pitch in and help.

So this book is full of light meals, main meals, side dishes and preserves for every home kitchen. (Wouldn't it be lovely to have a permanent stock of good pickles and lemon butter!) There's comforting family food, and soups to warm souls. Vegetarian dishes are included, as are my personal favourites, the tea time treats of my childhood – biscuits, cakes and slices.

From Cairns to Coolangatta, and Mt Isa to Mackay, this year has seen devastation we never thought possible: the freakish wall of water in Toowoomba, the floods that wiped out streets in Ipswich and Brisbane, and Cyclone Yasi that teased North Queensland, before delivering the pelting rains that continue to leave their mark.

During it, though, we never lost hope, and the importance of community meant we volunteered in the thousands, marching down streets, carrying mops and buckets and gloves and good cheer – the weapons needed to counter both the tears and the torment. Along the way, we met new friends, and learnt we were all in this together. Anna Bligh, whose recipe for Vietnamese Chicken and Mint Salad is featured on page 70, led the state-wide response. But everyone pitched in. Alison Alexander's famous Ginger Cake (my listeners just love it!) is on page 161, and owner of Aria restaurant, Matt Moran – my cooking chef on alternating weeks – has dished up his own recipe for Beef Bourguignon.

There's also Jenny Woodward, ABC TV's weather presenter, who is as at home in the kitchen as she is delivering your nightly weather forecast. She jumped at the opportunity to join in, giving us a special chilli jam recipe. Golden Guitar winner Troy Cassar-Daley – who learnt firsthand how the floods could wreak havoc on your home – shares a fantastic pasta recipe, and international cricketing hero Matt Hayden felt honoured to include his pawpaw chicken and spinach dish.

Karen Simons is a mum in Graceville, Brisbane, and someone who has taught me about the silver lining hiding in the clouds that gathered over

Brisbane in January. She opened her home and her heart to strangers, inviting anyone and everyone to drop by for a hot cuppa and a slice of cake. She agreed to be part of my post-flood broadcast, but demanded first that I peel a bag of onions. She likes to roll up her sleeves, and makes sure everyone else does the same. You can read Karen's recipe for Chicken and Chorizo Bake on page 41. And the wonderful Danielle Crismani, who became a household name organising food treats during the flood with Baked Relief, passes on her recipe for Digella's Cupcakes on page 154.

By providing your recipes – many of them treasured family secrets or from your own family recipe books – you have helped create both a valuable kitchen collection and a means to rebuild those precious family moments around the dinner table. Thank you. Thank you also to all those mums and dads who offered up a recipe that was not included. Alison Alexander's job in choosing what went in, and what didn't, must have been awful.

The summer of 2011 has sorely tested many of us, but doing my job each day, you can't help but admire the resilience of those who are suffering, and the big hearts and generous spirit of those who want to help them. All the profits from *A Generous Helping* will go to the Premier's Disaster Relief Appeal, to help those across the state still trying to rebuild their lives.

Thank you to Alison Alexander for her passion and her talent; to Jo Mackay for leading us; to the ABC's Tony Rasmussen and Theresa Rockley-Hogan for getting it started; and my winning ingredients – team-mates Rebecca Levingston, Halina Baczkowski, Terri Begley and Susan Walker. Thank you for opening your recipe books and allowing us to reproduce them for those who might have lost theirs. It's further proof of that silver lining. And thanks, Mum, and all the kitchen mums, who help build memories around the kitchen table each day. Enjoy.

Madonna King
612 ABC Brisbane

INTRODUCTION

My favourite childhood food memory is of coming home from boarding school to enjoy my mother's roast mutton and chocolate pudding – a simple meal repeated in households of the time around the country. It was many years later that I became interested in food and its provenance and this has been heightened through travelling and experiencing different ingredients and cultures.

Thankfully I have never been in the situation that so many Queenslanders suffered when their houses and businesses were flooded during the extraordinarily wet summer of 2010/2011. I can't imagine how awful this must be, but I did become aware of some of the distress it caused when assisting, along with so many others, in the ensuing cleanup. I regularly heard about books being lost and in particular cookbooks containing treasured recipes that had been handed down from one generation to another.

People who lost belongings during the floods were overwhelmed with offers of assistance from family, friends and complete strangers. It is well known that small communities pull together when times are tough and disaster prevails, but the spirit of generosity that existed in Brisbane following the floods is a memory I, and many others, will treasure. In a city of over a million people where neighbours sometimes don't know each other's names, so many people turned up wanting to lend a hand. The jobs were endless: from washing off the mud, trying to save precious photographs, cleaning crockery and washing mountains of clothes and linen to the small and large businesses whose offices were inundated with water, causing damage to equipment and office records.

The nurturing side of the human spirit was evident, with many people providing food for the work crews. Whole teams of people would cruise the suburbs handing out freshly made sandwiches and cakes of all descriptions. A baking frenzy took over the city for a few weeks and some of the recipes in this book were made during this time.

Following the flooding of Brisbane in January of 2011, I mentioned to Madonna King an idea I'd had to create a cookbook. She liked the idea and once the decision was made that the book would go ahead, Madonna challenged her listeners to send in their favourite recipes and another flood began – this time made up of emails and letters. As the emails arrived I would regularly head off to the kitchen to try out a new version of an old favourite.

I was constantly touched by the recipes that came with stories of where and how they had originated, and what memories the recipe held for the donor, and many of these stories have been included in this book. To me, the most moving of all was the recipe sent in by Shirley Graham for Hester's Boiled Fruit Cake. Shirley made this cake for her husband, Gordon, when he was serving in Vietnam, and now makes it for her son Stuart, who is in the armed services in the Middle East. Also included are an unusual recipe for Cream of Peanut Soup from Jo Belfield, as well as basic standbys such as Pikelets, Sultana Scones and a prize-winning Lemon Curd.

The job of collating the recipes into sections and then making the final choices was much more difficult than I had imagined due to the overwhelming response. Some people sent in one treasured recipe while others sent in their family's precious collection. The final choice of recipes was made for balance in the book and unfortunately, many were not included because I had already received a similar recipe, or due to lack of space.

I have a great interest in the food that is grown locally and admire the tenacity of Queensland farmers, graziers and fishermen during this past summer. Many saw months of hard work devastated by flooding or destroyed by Cyclone Yasi. However, fields and pastures will ultimately benefit from the soaking, and consumers will be the winners as production recovers.

My fortnightly visits to 612 ABC Brisbane to do my session with Madonna King are filled with laughter, learning and the joy of working with a great professional team. Madonna is always willing to try out new flavours and ingredients in the dishes that I bring in to the studio and I am grateful for her encouragement. I would like to thank Jo Mackay and Kylie Mason from HarperCollins*Publishers* for their assistance and patience in the development of this book.

As I write this, life has returned to normal after last summer, and it can be hard to find signs that the Brisbane River flooded. However, for many of those affected by flooding or cyclones, full recovery may take years rather than months. I hope this book will be a reminder of the generosity of spirit that was shown during this time and that it will become part of the social history of Brisbane of 2011.

Alison Alexander

LIGHT MEALS

CAULIFLOWER, LEEK AND BACON SOUP

This is my version of a soup we enjoyed when we lunched at the Rising Sun Hotel, Auburn in South Australia, during the winter of 2003.

1 tablespoon olive oil
4 leeks, white part only, sliced
1 medium onion, finely chopped
6 rashers bacon, rind removed and chopped
1 large cauliflower, chopped
2L (8 cups) chicken stock
2 tablespoons chopped parsley

Heat oil in a large pot and cook leeks, onion and bacon until the vegetables have softened. Add cauliflower and chicken stock and bring to the boil, then simmer, covered, for about 20 minutes or until the cauliflower is soft.

Puree in batches in a blender or food processor until smooth. Return soup to the pot and reheat, stirring constantly. Ladle soup into serving bowls and top with parsley.

Note: This soup can be frozen for up to 2 months.

Joan Bowman, Carseldine

CHICKEN SOUP FOR THE SOUL

My mum used to make this for us in the 70s and, with a few small changes, it still has the mmm effect 30 years later. The rosemary in this recipe is the magic ingredient.

1–1½kg chicken pieces, or a small whole chicken, skin removed
1 large onion, sliced
2 sprigs of fresh rosemary
2 large carrots, cubed
1 cup frozen peas
2 large potatoes, cubed
9 chicken stock cubes or equivalent chicken stock powder
440g tin cream of chicken soup

Place chicken in a large soup pot with sliced onions, rosemary sprigs and enough hot water to three-quarters fill the pot. Bring to the boil then reduce heat and simmer for 1 hour or until chicken is tender.

Remove chicken from pot and set aside to cool. Add all the vegetables and stock cubes and return to the boil. Simmer for about 20 minutes or until vegetables are just tender.

Remove chicken meat from bones in chunks and add to pot. Add the cream of chicken soup and stir gently to combine. Simmer a further 5 minutes, then check seasoning and adjust if necessary with a pinch of ground white pepper.

Nicola Booth, Woodford

CHORBA

(Tomato Soup with ras el hanout and noodles)

This soup is so easy to make even though it looks 'busy'; it has a lovely flavour and freezes beautifully. It always reminds me of large gatherings, lots of laughter and good times. The recipe came from a Moroccan cooking demonstration at the Wesley Hospital many years ago.

3 tablespoons olive oil
2 onions, chopped
2 cloves garlic, finely chopped
1 small butternut pumpkin, peeled and cut into small chunks
4 celery stalks, chopped
2 carrots chopped
1 large tin tomatoes, crushed
1 tablespoon tomato paste
4 cloves
2 teaspoons ras el hanout (see Note)
1 teaspoon cinnamon
1 teaspoon turmeric
2 teaspoons honey or sugar
1.8L (4¾ cups)vegetable stock
50g (½ cup) small pasta or broken vermicelli
lemon juice for taste
¼ cup chopped fresh coriander

Heat oil in a large saucepan and cook vegetables over medium heat until they begin to colour a little. Add tinned tomatoes and paste, spices, honey and stock and simmer gently, covered, for 30 minutes.

Add pasta and cook, uncovered, for a further 15 minutes. Add lemon juice to taste and stir in the coriander before serving.

Note: Ras el hanout is available in the spice aisle of most supermarkets.

Lyn Barber, Kenmore

COLD CUCUMBER AND PRAWN SOUP

2 cucumbers, peeled, de-seeded and chopped
500g (2 cups) natural yoghurt
50g cooked prawns
¼ onion, finely chopped
¼ cup mint leaves
1 clove garlic, finely chopped
250g (1 cup) sour cream
500ml (2 cups) chicken stock
salt and pepper

Have all ingredients well chilled before making this soup.

Place cucumber, yoghurt, prawns, onion, mint and garlic in a blender and process until smooth. Add sour cream, chicken stock and seasoning and blend again.

Pour into bowls and garnish with a sprig of mint.

Hazel Grebert, Carina Heights

CREAM OF PEANUT SOUP

The house parents at a boarding school for missionaries'
children used to serve this on Fridays. There was never
enough for seconds.

60g (¼ cup) butter
1 onion, chopped
2 stalks celery, chopped
3 tablespoons plain flour
2L (8 cups) chicken stock
500g (2 cups) smooth peanut butter
435ml (1¾ cups) cream
3 tablespoons chopped roasted peanuts

Melt butter in a large saucepan and sauté the onion and celery until the onion is transparent and golden. Stir in the flour and cook for 1 minute. Add the stock, stirring constantly, and bring to the boil.

Pass the mixture through a sieve and return to the saucepan, or puree with a hand blender. Add the peanut butter and cream and stir over low heat – do not allow to boil.

Ladle soup into bowls and garnish with peanuts.

Note: Evaporated milk can be used in place of the cream if preferred.

Jo Belfield, Bellbowrie

CREAM OF PUMPKIN SOUP

This soup is quick and my kids love it. The recipe was given to me by my dear friend Barbara, who now has MS. I am entering the recipe in honour of her and all the great recipes she has given me over the years.

2 tablespoons butter or oil
1 onion, chopped
1 tablespoon flour
1½ teaspoons curry powder
1L (4 cups) water
3 chicken stock cubes
500g pumpkin, cubed
1 teaspoon brown sugar
pinch nutmeg
salt and pepper
250ml (1 cup) milk or cream
chopped chives or parsley

Heat butter and sauté the onion until softened. Stir in flour and curry powder and cook for 1 minute. Gradually stir in water and crumbled chicken stock cubes.

Add pumpkin, brown sugar, nutmeg, and salt and pepper, then bring to the boil and simmer until pumpkin is tender. Puree the soup in batches in a blender or food processor then return to the pot. Add milk or cream and reheat gently, ensuring that the soup does not boil.

Ladle the soup into bowls and garnish with chives or parsley.

Christine Murphy, Tarragindi

CURRIED PARSNIP AND POTATO SOUP

This is my very favourite soup and the recipe is from my friend Carmel.

50g (¼ cup) butter
200g (1½ cups) chopped leek, white parts only
120g (¾ cup) chopped parsnips
240g (1⅔ cups) chopped carrots
2 bacon rashers, rind removed and chopped
2 teaspoons mild curry powder or more if desired
600g (roughly 4 medium) peeled and chopped potatoes
2 bay leaves
¼ teaspoon ground turmeric
1¼L (5 cups) chicken or vegetable stock
1 tablespoon chopped fresh parsley

Heat butter in a large pot and add leek, parsnips, carrots and bacon. Cook, stirring, for about 10 minutes until leek is soft but not browned. Add curry powder and continue to cook until fragrant. Add potatoes, bay leaves, turmeric and stock and simmer, covered, until potatoes are tender.

Discard the bay leaves and puree the mixture in batches in a blender or food processor until smooth. Return the soup to pot and simmer, stirring, until heated through.

Ladle soup into bowls sprinkled with parsley.

Note: Omit the bacon in this recipe to make it suitable for vegetarians. This soup can be made up to 3 days ahead and can be frozen.

Jan Rhoades, Upper Mt Gravatt

CURRY CRAB AND TOMATO SOUP

This recipe is absolutely delicious and so easily made.

400g tin tomato soup
400g tin tomatoes
170g tin crab meat
1 dessertspoon curry powder
1 dessertspoon finely chopped parsley

Using a blender, process tomato soup with tinned tomatoes and their liquid and strain puree through a sieve. Pour into a saucepan and heat to almost boiling.

Add the curry powder, crab and parsley to soup – reserving 4 teaspoons crab and 1 teaspoon parsley for garnish – and stir to combine.

Ladle the soup into bowls and add the reserved crab and parsley to the centre of each serving.

Note: A 170g tin prawns, chopped, can be used instead of the crab meat.

Terry Simpson, Brighton

Izzy's Yunion Soup

This soup was named 'Yunion' because my niece could not pronounce 'onion' when she was little.

This high-flavour classic soup recipe can be made easily at home. It is impressive at a dinner party and perfect as a midweek meal in a bowl.

I am submitting this recipe in honour of the Lockyer Valley being an onion growing district.

50g unsalted butter
1 tablespoon extra virgin olive oil
3 large onions, thinly sliced
2 garlic cloves, crushed
1 tablespoon plain flour
1L (4 cups) beef or chicken stock
600ml (2⅓ cups) dry white wine
1 fresh bay leaf
2 sprigs of thyme
coarse salt
freshly ground black pepper
1 baguette or other white bread, sliced
175g (1⅓ cups) freshly grated gruyère cheese

Put the oil and butter in a large saucepan and melt over a medium heat. Add the onions and cook over a low heat for 15–20 minutes or until soft.

Add the garlic and flour and cook, stirring, for about 1 minute. Add the stock, wine, bay leaf and thyme. Boil for 1 minute, lower the heat and simmer very gently for 20 minutes. Season to taste.

At this point, the soup will be cooked but standing time will improve its flavour so leave on a low heat for at least 30 minutes.

Before serving, preheat the grill. Put the bread slices on a baking tray and brown until lightly toasted. Set aside.

To serve, ladle the soup into ovenproof bowls and top with a few toasted bread slices. Sprinkle with cheese and heat under the grill until the cheese is browned and bubbling.

Serve immediately.

Nola Murphy, Beerwah

PEA AND HAM SOUP

This particular soup has become an annual event made with the remains of the Christmas ham. I am never bothered about being too accurate with measurements for this recipe as it is always good.

440g (2 cups) split peas
leftover ham bone
140g (1 cup) chopped celery with leaves
80g (½ cup) chopped onion
80g (½ cup) chopped carrots
1 clove garlic, crushed
1 bay leaf
1 teaspoon sugar
2 tablespoons butter
salt and pepper to taste
2 tablespoons flour (optional)

Wash and soak the peas overnight.

Drain peas, reserving the water. Place the reserved water in a large pot and add fresh water to make 2½ litres. Place peas and ham bone in the pot and cook gently for 2½ hours.

Add celery, onions, carrots, garlic, bay leaf and sugar and simmer for another 30 minutes. Add the butter and stir to dissolve.

If the soup needs thickening, blend the flour with a little water and stir in.

Joan Bowman, Carseldine

PEA SOUP

1 tablespoon butter
1 leek, white part only, chopped
2 potatoes, chopped
1¼L (5 cups) chicken stock
390g (3 cups) frozen peas

Melt butter in a large saucepan and cook the leek for 5 minutes, stirring until softened. Add potato and cook for 2 minutes. Add stock and bring to boil then reduce the heat and simmer, covered, for 10 minutes. Add peas and simmer for a further 10 minutes, or until vegetables are tender.

Puree soup in batches in a blender or food processor until smooth. Return the soup to the saucepan and reheat before serving.

Keiran Darby, Jindalee

QUICK ASIAN NOODLE SOUP

1L (4 cups) chicken stock
3 cloves garlic, sliced
2 tablespoons soy sauce
1½ tablespoons rice wine vinegar
few drops sesame oil
2 chicken breasts, skin off and sliced
100g (1 cup) dried rice vermicelli noodles
2 green onions, finely chopped
90g (1 cup) bean sprouts
coriander leaves
sambal oelek

Bring stock to the boil in a medium saucepan. Add garlic, soy, rice wine vinegar and sesame oil along with chicken slices and simmer until chicken is cooked through.

While soup is simmering, soak vermicelli in boiling water in large bowl for about 5 minutes. Drain the noodles and divide between four soup bowls. Ladle soup over vermicelli and top with green onions, sprouts, coriander and sambal oelek and serve immediately.

Note: For a vegetarian option, use vegetable stock, omit the chicken and use 2–3 cups diced vegetables.

Robyn Foster, Mount Cotton

AUSSIERONI

I originally made this recipe out of leftovers when my sons were small, and 35 years later they now cook it for themselves – and their children.

500g (5 cups) small pasta e.g. bows or macaroni
1 tablespoon butter or oil
1 onion, chopped
1 small capsicum, chopped
4 rashers bacon, rind removed, chopped
130g (1 cup) frozen peas
150g (1 cup) grated mature cheddar cheese
2 tomatoes, cut into wedges
chopped chives to garnish

Cook pasta in a large pot of boiling salted water.

Heat butter in frying pan and sauté the onion, capsicum and bacon until the onion is soft. Add peas and stir until defrosted.

Drain pasta when cooked and combine with bacon mixture and cheese. Serve immediately garnished with tomato wedges and chopped chives.

Marion Rodgers, Dayboro

CHICKEN AND NOODLE STIR-FRY WITH OYSTER SAUCE

You can use whatever vegetables are in season and inexpensive, or any vegetables you have in the refrigerator, sliced thinly.

2 tablespoons oil
5 chicken thigh fillets, cut into thin strips
1 onion, sliced
3 cloves garlic, minced
2½cm piece of ginger, skin removed and grated
2 carrots, thinly sliced
1 head broccoli, cut into small florets and stem thinly sliced
2 sticks celery, sliced
2 handfuls green beans, cut into 5cm lengths
1 red capsicum, cut into thin strips
1 packet fresh Udon noodles (see Note)
125ml (½ cup) oyster sauce
2 tablespoons soy sauce
1 tablespoons honey

Heat oil in a wok over high heat. Add chicken strips and cook lightly until coloured. Remove chicken and set aside.

Add more oil if necessary and stir-fry the onions, garlic and ginger for 1 minute.

Add all remaining vegetables to the wok with the chicken meat and stir-fry for a further 6–8 minutes. Add warmed noodles, oyster and soy sauces and honey and stir-fry for a few minutes.

Note: Udon noodles vary between brands so cook according to directions on the packet.

Nicola Booth, Woodford

PENNE ALLA CAPRESE

This recipe was taught to me by a friend in Italy and has become a family favourite in my house.

2 punnets cherry or grape tomatoes, cut in half
2 balls buffalo mozzarella, torn into bite-size pieces
175g (1 cup) green olives
2 cloves garlic, finely chopped
125ml (½ cup) extra virgin olive oil
30g (1 cup) basil, finely chopped
sea salt to taste
500g (5 cups) penne rigate

Mix tomatoes, mozzarella, olives, garlic, oil, basil and salt in a large bowl.
    Cook the pasta in a large pot of salted boiling water until al dente. Drain pasta and add to the tomato mixture, stirring to combine.

Eva Staunton, Ferny Hills

PRAWN PASTA

On a trip to New York last year doing some shows with Tommy Emmanuel, we ended up in beautiful Little Italy, which is a great part of New York. We stumbled upon one of the most authentic Italian places, and when I had this pasta I had to ask for the recipe. This is how it was explained it to me: 'Put the pasta onto boil, clean and chop the prawns, and add a little butter, white wine, garlic and red pepper.'

It was delicious; I have made this simple recipe many times since, and it always brings back memories of that day. Since you chop the prawns anyway, don't buy the large expensive kind. Small to medium sized are just fine and have more flavour, I reckon!

500g (5 cups) spaghetti
60ml (¼ cup) olive oil
500g medium green prawns, peeled and deveined, coarsely chopped
3 cloves garlic, finely chopped
dried chilli flakes to taste
salt and pepper
125g (½ cup) butter
250ml (1 cup) dry white wine
¼ cup parsley

Cook the pasta in a large pot of salted boiling water to al dente.

Heat olive oil in a large frying pan and sauté the prawns, garlic, dried chilli flakes and seasoning until prawns change colour, then set aside. Add butter and wine to the pan and increase the heat to allow the liquid to reduce by half.

Drain the pasta, reserving about ⅔ cup of the pasta water. Add the prawns, parsley and pasta to the pan and stir through. Cook the pasta and sauce over high heat for 2 minutes adding some of the pasta water if the mixture is dry.

Serve immediately with extra parsley sprinkled on top.

Troy Cassar-Daley

Ricotta and Spinach Stuffed Pasta Shells

32 extra large pasta shells
1 tablespoon olive oil
2 cloves garlic
500g spinach
600g (2⅓ cups) ricotta
600ml (2⅓ cups) tomato pasta sauce
500ml (2 cups) vegetable stock
1 tablespoon finely grated Parmesan cheese

Preheat oven to 180°C. Lightly oil a large dish, such as a lasagne dish.

Cook pasta in a large pot of boiling salted water for 3 minutes, then drain and allow to cool slightly.

Heat oil in a large frying pan and add garlic and spinach. Cook the mixture only until the spinach wilts then remove from the heat and squeeze out excess moisture from the spinach. Combine spinach and garlic with the ricotta in a large mixing bowl and spoon mixture into the cooled pasta shells.

Combine tomato sauce and stock in the lasagne dish and place pasta shells on top. Sprinkle with the Parmesan and cover the dish with foil.

Bake for 1 hour, removing foil for the last 15 minutes.

Note: 50g (½ cup) finely grated Parmesan cheese can be added to the ricotta mixture.

Keiran Darby, Jindalee

SMOKED SALMON PASTA WITH PINE NUTS, BASIL AND CHILLI

This dish I have created is an absolute favourite of mine and my husband's. One of the great things about it is that it doesn't take long to make. Complement it with a lovely summer salad with Parmesan cheese, grated carrots and pine nuts sprinkled on top. It is a dish that can be enjoyed throughout the year and is great with red or white wine. For me this recipe sums up my personality: quick, fresh, hot and with great taste! I believe this dish is foolproof and is ideal for those who love pasta and seafood. This special dish is always guaranteed to make me feel warm and fuzzy.

You can very the amount of the spices, if you like – I believe the amount of spice used can be so individual. I highly recommend using fresh tomatoes, basil, garlic and chilli for this dish. I also recommend using a good quality Parmesan cheese. This dish tastes best if served immediately. Enjoy!

1 tablespoon avocado oil
2 cloves garlic, crushed
1 red chilli, finely chopped
½ cup fresh basil, shredded
4 tomatoes, skinned and sliced, or 400g tin diced tomatoes
salt and pepper
½ teaspoon ground sweet paprika
1 teaspoon sugar
40g (¼ cup) pine nuts, ground
25g (¼ cup) finely grated Parmesan cheese
60ml (¼ cup) cream
½ teaspoon ground chilli

500g angel hair pasta
60g smoked salmon, cut into strips

Heat avocado oil in a pan and cook garlic, chilli and basil for 1 minute. Add tomatoes, seasoning, paprika, sugar and pine nuts. Sprinkle in some Parmesan cheese and add the cream and allow to simmer for about 10–15 minutes. Taste dish and add chilli if desired.

Meanwhile cook the pasta in a large pot of boiling salted water. When pasta is cooked, drain and combine with the sauce and smoked salmon.

Serve immediately with extra basil leaves, grated Parmesan cheese and cracked pepper.

Monica Bardini, Darra

Tagliatelle with Pumpkin, Pine nuts and Basil

500g tagliatelle
60ml (¼ cup) olive oil
2 tablespoons butter
1kg pumpkin, thinly sliced
1 large onion, finely diced
3 cloves garlic, crushed
250ml (1 cup) cream
155g (1 cup) pine nuts, toasted
45g (½ cup) freshly grated pecorino cheese
½ cup fresh basil leaves, chopped
1 teaspoon grated nutmeg

Cook tagliatelle in a large pot of boiling salted water until al dente.

Heat oil and butter in a large frying pan, add pumpkin and cook until just tender. Add onions and cook until soft, then add crushed garlic and stir well. Add cooked pasta and remaining ingredients and stir until combined and heated through.

Serve immediately with extra pecorino cheese.

Janet Carswell, Tallai

BLUE CHEESE AND TOMATO TART

I have always loved Roquefort cheese. On a trip to France I saw a signpost to Roquefort and went to check it out, very excited. It turns out there are two Roqueforts in France and only one makes cheese. After this great disappointment I found a French recipe book which contained several Roquefort recipes. The recipe I have included is the result of poor translation and guesswork. I have tried it with various Australian blue cheeses and it's always worked well, King Island Roaring Forties being the best.

1 sheet frozen shortcrust pastry, thawed
400g blue cheese
170ml (⅔ cup) cream
4–5 sprigs thyme, leaves stripped
pinch ground white pepper
1 large or 2 small ripe tomatoes, sliced
3 sprigs thyme, extra

Preheat oven to 180°C. Line a 23cm tart tin with the thawed shortcrust pastry and blind bake for 15 minutes. Remove from the oven and allow to cool. Reduce oven to 170°C.

Mash together the cheese and cream, stirring in the thyme leaves and pepper. Pour mixture into the tart base and cover with slices of tomato. Top with thyme sprigs and bake in 170°C oven for 20–25 minutes. The tomatoes should just be softening and the cheese filling starting to become golden.

Remove the tart from the oven and allow to cool to room temperature before serving with a rocket salad.

Terry Straight, Hawthorne

GOAT'S CHEESE AND TAPENADE TART WITH RUSTIC TOMATO SAUCE

When I first made this recipe, I discovered that goat's cheese is made right here in south east Queensland and I now use it a lot more. This luncheon dish is best accompanied by a salad, good wine and wonderful friends.

PASTRY
150g (1 cup) plain flour
160g (⅔ cup) butter, chopped
1 egg yolk
1 tablespoon lemon juice
3 tablespoons iced water

FILLING
150g (⅔ cup) olive tapenade
150g goat's cheese, thinly sliced
cracked pepper
4 eggs, lightly beaten
250ml (1 cup) cream
125ml (½ cup) milk
½ teaspoon sweet paprika

Preheat oven to 180°C.

Sift flour into a mixing bowl and rub in the butter until mixture resembles dry breadcrumbs. Combine egg yolk, lemon juice and water and mix into dry ingredients to form a firm dough, adding more water if necessary. The pastry could also be made in a food processor.

Shape the dough into a disc, wrap in plastic and refrigerate for 30 minutes.

Roll dough out to line a 23cm flan tin and blind bake for 15 minutes then remove from the oven and cool slightly.

For the filling, spread the olive tapenade evenly over the base of the pastry case. Place cheese slices on top and sprinkle with cracked pepper. Whisk eggs, cream and milk together and gently pour over the cheese then sprinkle with the paprika.

Place tin on an oven tray and bake in the oven for 40–45 minutes. Serve hot with Rustic Tomato Sauce.

Note: A good quality sour cream pastry is available at some delicatessens and could be used for this tart.

Rustic Tomato Sauce
2 tablespoons olive oil
2 onions, peeled and chopped
3 cloves garlic, crushed with a little salt
125ml (½ cup) dry red wine
250g (about 2 whole) ripe tomatoes, peeled, seeded and roughly
    chopped
1 teaspoon finely chopped oregano
1 teaspoon finely chopped thyme
3 tablespoons finely chopped basil
salt
freshly ground black pepper

Heat the oil in a large heavy-based frying pan. Add onion and garlic and cook until softened.

Add wine, tomatoes, herbs and seasoning and simmer for 20 minutes until the sauce thickens.

Anne Armansin, The Gap

Nicoise Salad a la Yvette

2 medium potatoes
2 eggs, at room temperature
100g green beans, tails removed
8–10 baby cos lettuce leaves
1 large tomato, cut into wedges
½ cucumber, peeled and sliced
200g tin tuna or salmon, drained
3–4 anchovy fillets, drained on a paper towel and sliced in half
    lengthways
1 teaspoon tiny capers
6–8 stuffed green olives, cut in half
2 tablespoons chopped basil

Dressing
1 egg yolk
1 teaspoon smooth Dijon mustard
salt and pepper
125ml (½ cup) olive oil
juice from half a lemon
1 clove garlic, crushed

For the dressing, whisk the egg yolk, Dijon mustard and salt and pepper in a bowl. Slowly drizzle the olive oil over the mixture while whisking vigorously at the same time. The mixture will emulsify but if it starts to separate, stop adding the oil and continue to whisk until it blends together again.

Finally add the lemon juice and garlic and check seasoning.

For the salad, boil the potatoes with their skins on and, when almost cooked through, add the eggs and cook for 5 minutes until soft-boiled.

Remove from the heat and run the eggs under cold water to stop them cooking, then peel the eggs and cut in half.

Cut potatoes into quarters, remove the skin then cut into bite-size pieces, and pour over enough dressing to coat.

Steam the beans for 5 minutes and then rinse with cold water and drain.

Arrange all the salad ingredients in a large bowl and drizzle with the remaining dressing. Sprinkle with freshly chopped basil.

Yvette Polonyi, Harrison

TUNA SLICE

Easy to make and everyone who has tasted it wants the recipe. Even the grandchildren will eat it!

250g packet cheese biscuits
125g (½ cup) butter, melted
2 eggs, lightly beaten
375ml (1½ cups) evaporated milk
425g tin tuna, drained
70g (½ cup) chopped celery
1 medium onion, chopped
1 teaspoon English mustard
½ teaspoon salt
¼ teaspoon pepper
¼ teaspoon cayenne pepper

Preheat oven to 180°C. Lightly grease a 16cm x 26cm slice tin.

Place biscuits in a food processor and process until finely chopped. Add melted butter and process until only just combined. Press into slice tin.

Combine all remaining ingredients in a mixing bowl and pour over the biscuit base.

Bake for 35 minutes or until set.

Kay Hams, Ferny Grove

WELSH RAREBIT

My late mother was of Welsh descent and this is one of my favourite meals that she made. When my children were young and went to visit Ma, they always asked her to make it as it is their favourite too. I still make it for them and my grandchildren and I never seem to be able to make enough, as they always come back for seconds.

125–250g (1–2 cups) grated tasty cheese
enough milk to cover the cheese
salt and pepper to taste
2–4 eggs, lightly beaten

Place the cheese, milk, salt and pepper in a double-boiler over medium heat and stir until the cheese melts. Remove from the heat and stir in the eggs. Ensure the eggs are well combined to avoid white specks.

Return to the heat and stir continuously until the mixture thickens. Do not allow the mixture to boil.

Serve immediately on crisp toast at any time of the day.

Kay Galbraith, Yamanto

MAIN MEALS

AUNTIE ANNE'S SPECIAL CHRISTMAS HAM

*Christmas is all about family and this ham is cooked
each year and shared by my family.*

80g (⅓ cup, firmly packed) brown sugar
90g (⅓ cup) wholegrain mustard
105g (⅓ cup) red currant jelly
1 leg of ham
20–30 whole cloves
2 stubbies of beer

Preheat the oven to 180°C.

Combine the sugar, mustard and jelly in a small bowl and set aside.

Cut through the rind of the ham, about 10cm from the shank end, in a
zigzag pattern. To remove the rind, slip a blunt knife around the edge and
pull the rind away from the fat. Cut through the fat in a diamond pattern
and place a clove in the centre of each diamond.

Place ham on a rack in a baking dish and brush the ham with about a
third of the sugar mixture and then pour over the beer. Cover the shank end
of the ham with foil and bake for 1½ hours, basting with the remaining
glaze a few times.

Sian Weston, Wurtulla

BABOOTIE

I got this recipe from my nephew Rob's Aunty Trixie while in Durban, South Africa, in 2005 for his marriage to my niece Natasha. Aunt Trixie was 83 at the time and so full of life. Unfortunately, she has now passed away, but this recipe brings back so many good memories every time I cook it. It has become a favourite in our family.

2½cm-thick slice of wholemeal bread
300ml (1¼ cup) milk
2 tablespoons vegetable oil
2 onions, sliced into rings
1kg lean beef mince
1 tablespoon curry powder
1 tablespoon brown sugar
pinch salt
½ teaspoon pepper
1 teaspoon turmeric
5 teaspoons white vinegar
60g (½ cup) sultanas
3 tablespoons mild fruit chutney
3 eggs, lightly beaten

Preheat oven to 180°C.

Place bread in a bowl, cover with the milk and set aside until soft.

Heat oil in a large saucepan and sauté onions until golden. Add mince and cook until lightly browned – do not overcook.

Squeeze milk out of bread, reserving milk, and add bread to the mince. Add all remaining ingredients except the reserved milk and eggs and stir to combine. Spoon into a large overproof dish.

Beat the eggs and milk together and pour gently over the mince mixture. Bake, uncovered, for 30–40 minutes or until the egg mixture has set. Serve with turmeric rice and steamed vegetables.

VARIATION:

Spread almond flakes or onion rings on top of milk and egg mixture before placing in the oven.

Pam Bazzo, Paddington

BEEF BIRDS

This recipe was given to us by an American exchange student who stayed with us many years ago. I've made it many times for friends and family and everyone loves it.

1½kg round steak
salt and pepper
3 rashers bacon, rind removed and finely chopped
1 medium onion, finely chopped
1 carrot, cut into batons
2 large dill pickles, slice thinly
1 tablespoon oil
1½ cups beef stock
1 tablespoon cornflour
2 tablespoons water

Cut the meat into 12 pieces, removing any fat, and flatten then pound with mallet. Sprinkle each piece of steak with salt and pepper. Onto each piece of meat place a teaspoonful each of bacon, onion, carrot and pickle. Roll up and secure with string or tooth picks.

Heat oil in a large pan and brown meat parcels on all sides. Add stock, cover and simmer for about an hour.

Combine the cornflour and water and stir into the pan to thicken the sauce.

Gai Aplin, Murrumba Downs

BEEF BOURGUIGNON

I really love to prepare slow-cooked meals as the smell wafts through the house while you're cooking. I then wait in anticipation for the first bite and the reward of each piece of beef melting in your mouth. This beef bourguignon recipe is a great, hearty dish to share with your family.

1kg chuck steak, cut into 5cm x 5cm cubes
750ml (3 cups) dry red wine
2 garlic cloves, crushed
10 sprigs of thyme
5 bay leaves
2 tablespoons vegetable oil
250g streaky bacon, cut into ½cm strips
30g button mushrooms, with stalks cut flush with mushroom cap
120g plain flour
1 tablespoon tomato paste
1½L veal stock
300g pearl onions, peeled
salt and pepper

Place the beef into a large bowl and pour the red wine over it. Add the garlic, thyme and bay leaves, cover with plastic wrap and refrigerate overnight. Next day, strain through a colander, reserving the wine. Place the beef on paper towel, pat dry to remove any excess liquid then return the thyme and bay leaves to the wine.

Preheat the oven to 140°C.

Heat 1 tablespoon vegetable oil in an ovenproof pot over medium heat and add the bacon. Cook for 3 minutes until golden brown and crisp, then remove and drain on kitchen paper. Set aside until required.

Add the mushrooms to the saucepan and cook for approximately 4 minutes until brown then remove and set aside until required.

Heat the second tablespoon of vegetable oil and when hot, add a third of the beef to the saucepan. Cook for 6–8 minutes until brown on all sides then set aside. Continue to cook the remaining beef in batches, adding more oil to the pan if required.

Once all of the meat has been browned, return it to the saucepan then sprinkle the flour over it. Stir to ensure that the meat is well coated then add the tomato paste and cook for a further 2 minutes stirring constantly. Pour in the reserved wine and herbs, increase the heat and bring to the boil. Cook for about 25 minutes until the liquid has reduced by half.

Add the veal stock, return to a simmer then reduce to a low heat and cook for 1 hour, stirring occasionally. Add the onions, bacon and mushrooms, cover with a lid and place in the oven. Cook for 2 hours, until the liquid has thickened and the meat is very tender. Remove from the oven, season with salt and pepper then serve with boiled new potatoes and green vegetables.

Matt Moran, chef

BEST EVER MEATLOAF

I got this recipe from a workmate 32 years ago when I was newly married and had no idea how to cook! I am still making it; it is my sons' favourite thing to eat, and everyone who has tried it just loves it.

1kg sausage mince
75g (¾ cup) breadcrumbs
90g (¾ cup) grated cheese
1 Granny Smith apple, peeled, grated and juice squeezed out
1 heaped teaspoon curry powder
1 egg, lightly beaten
2 onions, finely chopped
good shake dried parsley flakes
salt and pepper

Preheat oven to 180°C.

Put all ingredients into a large bowl and mix well with your hands to combine. Press into a 20cm x 28cm roasting dish and bake for 1½ hours.

This meatloaf can be eaten hot or cut into squares for a picnic.

Anne Semark, Little Mountain

CHICKEN AND CHORIZO BAKE

During the time of the flood we had many gatherings at my home and usually served up dinner to 20 or so friends, neighbours or family each evening by candlelight. (Even when the lights went back on I was forced to turn lights off – they decided they liked the effect!)

Anne and Dave Kuscopf were two of those special people for me during that time. Anne, I must confess, is my saviour here; this is her recipe. I pulled in a favour. I figured someone who once owned a deli and her own catering business was far better placed than me to provide something edible for print!

1 free range chicken, cut into 8 pieces
2 chorizo, or spicy Italian sausages, cut into 1cm pieces
1 garlic clove, crushed
½ onion, thinly sliced
1 red capsicum, cut in thick slices
1 yellow capsicum, cut in thick slices
450g tin Italian tomatoes, roughly chopped
60ml (¼ cup) white wine
salt and pepper
3–4 fresh bay leaves
small handful of black olives (optional)
3 tablespoons extra virgin olive oil

Preheat oven to 180°C.

Add chicken pieces, sausage, garlic, onion, capsicums, tomatoes and white wine to a large baking tray, season and toss to mix. Ensure the chicken pieces are skin side up, then add the bay leaves and olives and drizzle over the extra virgin olive oil.

Bake for 1¼ hours.

Karen Simons, Graceville

CRUSTY CHEESE HOT POT

My mother used to make this recipe and it's a great one-pot meal.

MEATBALLS

500g low fat mince
50g (½ cup) rolled oats
1 teaspoon dry mustard
1 egg, lightly beaten
1 teaspoon minced garlic
salt and pepper

HOT POT SAUCE

2 tablespoons butter or margarine
2 onions, chopped
2 carrots, sliced
2 tablespoons wholemeal plain flour
750ml (3 cups) beef stock
4 slices of French bread stick
60g (½ cup) grated tasty cheese

For the meatballs, combine all ingredients in a mixing bowl then roll into small balls. Refrigerate the meatballs while you make the sauce.

Melt butter in an ovenproof casserole dish and cook onion and carrot for 5 minutes. Stir in the flour and cook for 1 minute before adding stock and bring to the boil, stirring constantly.

Add the meatballs and simmer, covered, for 20 minutes.

Preheat the oven to 200°C.

Uncover the casserole dish and place the bread on top of the meatballs. Scatter over the cheese and bake in the oven until the cheese melts and is golden.

Note: Instead of using the oven, the casserole dish could be put under a preheated grill to melt the cheese.

Patricia McClafferty, The Gap

FASULYE

(Lamb and Bean Casserole)

I discovered this dish in Greece many years ago. It's hearty and comforting and delicious. It is said to have originated among shepherds on hillsides who combined tough old lamb with wild herbs to cook slowly over their fire overnight, ready for the next day.

I originally based this on a recipe in an old Sainsbury's cookbook in the UK, but have adapted it over the years and substituted fresh ingredients. You can use cheap cuts of lamb – the more fat, the tastier it gets – and the other ingredients are relatively inexpensive. The recipe is very adaptable and can be easily expanded for unexpected guests – just add more tomatoes and a can of haricots. All amounts are approximate in any case, and you can vary the ingredients according to preference. The dish can be frozen successfully.

It is one of my favourite recipes of all time!

450g (2¼ cups) dried haricot beans
500g lamb, e.g. neck fillet, shoulder or boned shank
1 tablespoon olive oil
2 large onions, sliced
3 cloves of garlic, peeled but left whole
2 tablespoons tomato puree
500ml (2 cups) vegetable stock
4 tablespoon oregano, chopped
salt and pepper

Cover haricot beans with water and soak overnight.

Cut the lamb into 3cm cubes. Heat the oil in a large saucepan over high heat and brown the lamb on all sides then set aside. Sauté the onion and garlic until the onion is translucent.

Drain and rinse the beans and add with the lamb to the tomato puree, vegetable stock and oregano. Season with salt and pepper and bring to the boil, then reduce the heat to a simmer and cook, covered, for 1½ hours or until the meat and beans are tender.

Serve with crusty bread to mop up the sauce.

Jude Garlick, Bulimba

GREEN CURRY OF CHICKEN

2 teaspoons peanut oil
1½ tablespoons green curry paste
1 onion, cut into wedges
750g chicken thigh fillets, cut into pieces
185ml (¾ cup) chicken stock
375ml (1½ cups) coconut milk
100g green beans, cut into 4cm lengths
2 kaffir lime leaves, very finely shredded
50g (⅓ cup) bamboo shoots
1 tablespoon fish sauce
2 teaspoons brown sugar
⅓ cup coriander leaves

Heat oil in a large saucepan over medium heat. Cook curry paste for 1 minute. Add onion and chicken pieces and cook for 3–4 minutes. Add stock and coconut milk and simmer for 15 minutes, covered.

Add beans, kaffir lime leaves, bamboo shoots, fish sauce and sugar and cook, uncovered, for 7 minutes or until the beans are just tender.

Stir through the coriander and serve with steamed jasmine rice.

Mary Rosenberg, Caboolture

IMPOSSIBLE PIE

2 bacon rashers, rind removed and diced
3 sliced spring onions, or 1 chopped onion
40g (⅓ cup) plain flour
375ml (1½ cups) milk
3 eggs, lightly beaten
130g tin corn kernels, drained
125g (1 cup) grated tasty cheese
2 tablespoons chopped parsley
pinch salt and pepper

Preheat oven to 180°C. Grease an oven-proof quiche dish.

Heat a non-stick frying pan and sauté the bacon until it has started to brown. Add the onion and continue to cook until it has softened, then set aside to cool.

Whisk flour with milk then add the eggs and mix well. Stir in bacon, onion, corn, cheese and parsley, season and pour mixture into prepared dish. Bake for 40 minutes or until set.

Serve with a salad.

Note: Tinned tuna or salmon can be substituted for the bacon.

Patricia Riddel, Elimbah

LAMB AND SPINACH CURRY

60ml (¼ cup) vegetable oil
2 medium onions, finely chopped
1kg diced lamb
1 teaspoon finely grated ginger
1 teaspoon finely chopped garlic
3 tablespoons tomato paste
2 teaspoons salt
2 teaspoons garam masala
1 teaspoon turmeric
1 teaspoon chilli powder
1 teaspoon ground coriander
1 teaspoon cumin
200g frozen spinach, thawed
250ml (1 cup) water

Heat oil in a large saucepan and cook the onions until dark golden. Add lamb and stir over high heat to brown the pieces. Add ginger, garlic and tomato paste and cook for 2 minutes before adding salt and spices and stirring to coat the meat.

Squeeze excess liquid out of the thawed spinach and add to the lamb with the water. Cook at a simmer, covered, until the lamb is tender.

Geeta Bhasin, Kenmore

MOTHER WOLFF SOUP

This recipe was passed onto me by my Jewish mother and is a meal in a bowl and wonderful for families as it serves 8–10 people, or 6 hungry teenagers.

1kg lean stewing steak, cut into large cubes
250g marrow bones, cut into 5cm sections
4L (16 cups) cold water
100g (½ cup) dried lima beans, soaked overnight
1 large onion, diced
1 cup each diced potatoes, carrots, celery, yellow or white squash,
    green beans, peas and parsnips
440g tin tomato puree
55g (¼ cup) each rice, barley and yellow split peas
salt and pepper to taste
80g (½ cup) small soup pasta or macaroni
½ cup finely chopped parsley or dill

Place steak, bones and water in a large pot and slowly bring to the boil. Simmer gently for 1 hour, skimming any froth that comes to the surface.

Drain the lima beans and add with the vegetables, tomato puree, rice and pulses to the stock and cook, covered, for a further 2 hours. Season with salt and pepper to taste then add pasta and cook, uncovered, for 20 minutes.

Ladle soup into bowls and garnish with parsley or dill.

Note: This soup will keep for 5 days in the refrigerator. Choko can also be used. Gravy beef is ideal for this recipe.

Heather Deane, Wynnum

MUSSEL SOUP

I love to cook. My wife and I go to restaurants and if she orders something that she finds very tasty she will give me one or two bites with instructions that I work out how to make the dish (or something similar). This is one such dish. I don't remember where we were but she ordered a mussel soup and I had a taste. It took a couple of attempts but I eventually came up with this recipe, which is a very nice mussel soup that is easy to make. You can exchange the prawns for crab pieces but it is fairly important to have the crustacean in there as part of the fun of this dish is that you kind of need to use fingers, which makes it a great social event for everyone eating with you.

1 tablespoon olive oil
4 cloves garlic, finely chopped
1L (4 cups) chicken stock
1kg mussels, de-bearded
300g scallops
300g salmon fillets, cut into 2cm cubes
12 whole green prawns, peeled and deveined
1 punnet cherry tomatoes, cut in half
1 bunch Italian parsley, roughly chopped

Heat the olive oil in a large saucepan and sauté the garlic until light golden. Add chicken stock and bring to the boil. Add seafood and cook, covered, for 5 minutes. Lastly, add the tomatoes and parsley and cook for a further 5 minutes.

Serve with fresh crusty bread.

Luke Grant, Strathpine

Pasties

This recipe is a favourite of mine, especially when my son Alex goes out for a long 100km training ride and walks in with a massive appetite – he can eat 4 of these pasties in one sitting!

Pastry
300g (2 cups) plain flour
300g (2 cups) self-raising flour
1 teaspoon salt
250g (1 cup) butter
1 teaspoon lemon juice
160–250ml (⅔–1 cup) water

Filling
500g minced beef
2 onions, finely chopped
2 potatoes, grated
2 carrots, grated
1 parsnip, grated
250g peas
pinch thyme leaves
2 crumbled beef stock cubes
salt
freshly ground pepper
1 egg, lightly beaten

Preheat oven to 200°C.

For the pastry, sift the flours and salt together and then place in a food processor. Add the chopped cold butter and process until the mixture resembles breadcrumbs. Add the lemon juice and, while it is still mixing, slowly add water until it starts turning into a ball of dough.

Turn the dough out onto a well-floured bench and knead lightly until smooth. Divide mixture into 12 portions and roll each portion of dough out to a circle, using a saucer as a cutting guide.

For the filling, combine the meat, vegetables and seasonings in a large bowl and stir until well mixed.

Spoon an equal amount of the filling onto the middle of each pastry circle. Brush halfway around each circle with water and join the edges together over the top. Squeeze and pinch along the join to make a nice pattern with your fingers. Place on a baking tray and prick each one a couple of times with a fork to let the steam escape while cooking.

Brush with a beaten the egg to give a golden glaze.

Bake for 10 minutes then reduce heat to 180°C for a further 30 minutes.

Evelyn Smyth, Ormond

PAWPAW CHICKEN AND SPINACH

Mark Tully (known affectionately as 'The Chicken Whisperer') along with many other friends from the Lockyer Valley, provided exceptional support and kindness to me throughout the production of my recent television show.

Naturally, I was devastated upon hearing the news that Mark and many of his neighbours in the area suffered such devastation and loss to their properties, their businesses, and for some even their families. I think the things that matter most when faced with hardship in times like these are the small things: a warm embrace from a friend or loved one; lending a supporting ear or a helping hand; and always the joy and comfort of sharing a good home-cooked meal.

This recipe was given to me by Mark when we first met and is one of my family's absolute favourites.

1–2 pawpaws, diced
500g chicken breast
handful of wattle seeds
4 lemon-scented myrtle leaves
60g (¼ cup) butter
olive oil
juice of ½ orange
pinch salt
1 clove garlic, chopped
2 handfuls of spinach leaves

Process the pawpaw in a food processor until you have a smooth paste. Place puree in a bowl and add the chicken. Marinate for a few hours; this helps to tenderise the chicken and create flavour.

Toast the wattle seeds for a few minutes in a pan then grind with a mortar and pestle and set aside. Lightly pound the lemon-scented myrtle leaves in the mortar and pestle.

Add butter and olive oil to a frying pan on medium heat. Add chicken and fry until golden brown – about 6 minutes each side. Sprinkle wattle seeds over chicken, then add leaves. Pour in orange juice and season with salt. Remove the chicken breasts from the pan and rest for 5 minutes.

In the same pan, fry off the garlic and two handfuls of spinach over high heat until the spinach has wilted.

To serve, place some spinach on the plate and top with chicken. Drizzle with a little olive oil and serve immediately.

Matt Hayden, former Australian cricketer

PESTO SALMON

2 pieces of fresh salmon fillet, skin off
handful of raw macadamia nuts
2 tablespoons good quality basil pesto

Preheat oven to 180°C.

Cut salmon in half lengthways and place on an oven tray lined with baking paper. Roughly chop the macadamia nuts into slightly smaller pieces, place in a bowl with the pesto and mix together. Spoon over the top of each piece of salmon.

Bake for approximately 15 minutes. Serve with steamed bok choy and mushrooms.

Note: There will be some pesto oil left on the baking paper that can be drizzled over the vegetables.

Gail Hargreaves, Currimundi

PORK WITH CHILLI AND CASHEWS

1 tablespoon peanut oil
300g pork fillet, sliced
1 clove garlic, chopped
1 small onion, cut into wedges
1 red capsicum, sliced
2 long red chillies, sliced
125g (1¼ cups) snow peas, trimmed and halved
2 green onions, sliced
1 tablespoon oyster sauce
2 tablespoons fish sauce
1½ tablespoons lime juice
3 teaspoons brown sugar
½ cup roughly chopped basil
40g (⅓ cup) roasted cashews

Heat half the oil in a wok and stir-fry pork in batches until golden. Remove from heat and set aside.

Add remaining oil to the wok and stir-fry garlic, onion, capsicum and chilli for 4 minutes or until onion is tender. Return the pork to the wok with the snow peas and green onions and cook for 3 minutes.

Combine oyster sauce, fish sauce, lime juice and sugar in a small bowl and pour into the wok, stirring continuously for 1 minute. Finally, toss through basil, top with cashews and serve with steamed jasmine rice.

Mary Rosenberg, Caboolture

QUICK BEEF CURRY

1 tablespoon vegetable oil
1 onion, diced
3 cloves garlic, crushed
1 capsicum, diced
500g extra lean mince
1 teaspoon crushed ginger
1 teaspoon turmeric
1½ teaspoons cumin
2 teaspoons beef stock powder
400g tin diced tomatoes
100g green beans, chopped
1 cup chopped mushrooms
½ teaspoon chilli powder

Heat some oil in a saucepan and sauté the onion, garlic and capsicum until the onion is transparent. Add the mince and stir until it is evenly browned.

Add the remaining ingredients, bring to the boil and simmer for 10 minutes.

Serve with corn chips and a bowl of sour cream.

Ann Earle, Sinnamon Park

SIMPLE MASSAMAN BEEF CURRY

2 tablespoons vegetable oil
600g cubed beef, trimmed of all fat
1 large onion, thinly sliced
210g bottle Thai-style massaman curry paste
4 fresh kaffir lime leaves
400ml tin coconut milk
2 teaspoons fish sauce
1 stalk of lemongrass, trim off grassy top, split down the middle
2 desiree potatoes, peeled and cut into chunks
1 carrot, peeled and chopped
130g (1 cup) fresh or frozen peas
2 tablespoons chopped fresh coriander
toasted peanuts for garnish

Heat 1 tablespoon oil in a large saucepan over high heat and brown the beef in batches then set aside.

Heat remaining oil in the pan then add the onion and sauté until it has softened. Add curry paste and lime leaves and cook for 30 seconds. Return meat to the pan, stir in the coconut milk, fish sauce and lemongrass and bring to the boil. Reduce the heat and simmer for 30 minutes, stirring occasionally.

Add the potatoes and carrot and continue to cook on low heat for a further 20 minutes. Stir in the peas and half the coriander and simmer for a final 5 minutes.

Serve with jasmine rice and garnish with remaining coriander and toasted peanuts.

Joan Jockel, The Gap

SRI LANKAN LAMB CURRY

This is one of our favourite home curries, especially because our 2-year-old son loves it!

1kg diced lamb
2 teaspoons chilli powder
1½ teaspoons salt
3 tablespoons soy sauce
3 tablespoons oil
1 onion, finely chopped
10 cloves garlic, minced
1 tablespoon ground coriander
1 tablespoon ground cumin
1 teaspoon black mustard seeds
1 teaspoon fenugreek seeds
1 teaspoon ground cardamom
1 teaspoon cinnamon powder
1cm piece rampe (optional – see Note)
2 tablespoons curry leaves
1 cup water
1 cup coconut milk

Place lamb in a bowl with chilli powder, salt and soy sauce and leave to marinate for 1 hour.

Heat oil in a large saucepan and add onion, garlic, spices and curry leaves and cook for a few minutes until onion is transparent. Add the marinated lamb and water, bring to the boil and cook, covered, on low heat for about 1 hour.

Stir in coconut milk and simmer, uncovered, for another 15 minutes.

Serve with steamed basmati rice.

Note: The individual spices can be substituted with 3 tablespoons Sri Lankan curry powder. Rampe is available in Asian and Indian stores.

Belinda Dennis, Alderley

SWEET LAMB CURRY

2 tablespoons oil
1 large onion, finely chopped
1 clove garlic, finely chopped
2–3 tablespoons curry powder or 2 tablespoons curry paste
70g (½ cup) fruit chutney
1 Granny Smith apple, peeled, cored and finely chopped
2 potatoes, diced
750g diced lamb
60g (½ cup) sultanas
375ml (1½ cups) beef stock or water

Heat oil in a large saucepan and cook onion and garlic for 3–4 minutes. Add curry powder or paste and chutney and stir until well combined. Add remaining ingredients and bring to the boil.

Reduce heat and simmer, uncovered, for 1¼ hours or until meat is tender and liquid has thickened.

ACCOMPANIMENTS FOR THE CURRY
Steamed rice
2 sliced bananas dipped in lemon juice and coated in desiccated
    coconut
Plain yoghurt
Sliced cucumber
Coriander leaves for garnish

Note: Beef can be used instead of the lamb.

Christine Murphy, Tarragindi

Sweet and Sour Meatballs

*My children and my grandchildren are in love with this
dish and I think they would eat it every day if allowed!*

Meatballs
500g lean beef mince
50g (¼ cup) brown or long grain rice
1 onion, grated
2 eggs, lightly beaten
1 tablespoon parsley, finely chopped
1 clove garlic, crushed
½ teaspoon salt
2 tablespoons vegetable oil

Sauce
400g tin tomato soup
60ml (¼ cup) cider vinegar
3 tablespoons brown sugar
1 cup celery, finely chopped
1 green capsicum, chopped

Combine all the meatball ingredients except the oil in a bowl and form into
balls the size of walnuts. Heat oil in a large frying pan and sauté until
browned on all sides – this may need to be done in batches.

For the sauce, combine all ingredients in a saucepan and simmer,
covered, for 20 minutes. Remove cover and simmer a further 5 minutes.
Add the meatballs to the sauce and heat through before serving on
spaghetti.

Variation:

Preheat oven to 180°C.

Cook some pasta shells in salted water until tender. Drain the pasta and place half in the bottom of a greased casserole dish. Top with browned meatballs then cover with the remaining pasta.

Pour over the sauce and bake for 20 minutes.

Heather Deane, Wynnum

TAHITIAN COCONUT CHICKEN

This recipe is one of our family's favourites when it comes to entertaining. It's often requested for birthday and family celebrations. The sauce can be prepared ahead and the chicken can easily be kept warm awaiting your guests. It never fails to please – the flavours are a winning combination. The chicken remains moist and the fruit complements it beautifully. Served with a salad or fresh steamed vegetables you simply can't go wrong. It can be enjoyed in all seasons.

1 egg
4 skinless chicken breasts
60g (½ cup) plain flour
60g (1 cup) shredded coconut
60g (¼ cup) butter
1 tablespoon oil
30g butter, extra
1 teaspoon curry powder
250ml (1 cup) chicken stock
80g (½ cup) seeded raisins, chopped
1 apple, peeled, quartered and thinly sliced
1 banana, sliced
125ml (½ cup) natural yoghurt
2 teaspoons brandy

Beat egg in a shallow bowl. Lightly dust chicken breasts in flour and dip into the egg and then into the coconut; set aside.

Heat butter and oil in a frying pan and cook the chicken on both sides until cooked through and golden. Remove from the pan, rest on kitchen paper and keep warm.

Melt extra butter and curry powder in the frying pan. Add remaining ingredients except the yoghurt and brandy and cook for 3 minutes or until the fruit softens. Lastly, stir in the yoghurt and brandy and heat through.

Place chicken on serving plates, spoon over the sauce and serve immediately.

Frances Golding, Robertson

TERRIFIC THAI LAMB CURRY

This recipe has evolved in our home over the years by experimenting with a whole variety of Thai curries. Apart from it being a crowd pleaser, the two main things I love about it are that it's completely reliable and it only takes 45 minutes to cook.

2 tablespoons peanut oil
600g lamb leg steaks, cut into 3cm pieces
1 red onion, chopped
1 teaspoon ground cumin
3 tablespoons Thai red curry paste
3 kaffir lime leaves
2 tablespoons satay sauce
1 cinnamon stick
400ml tin coconut milk
250ml (1 cup) water
1 tablespoon fish sauce
250g sweet potato, chopped into 4cm pieces

Heat oil in wok or large pan on high heat and brown the lamb in batches, then remove and set aside.

Reduce heat to medium and sauté the onion and cumin, stirring occasionally, until softened. Stir in the curry paste and cook for 1–2 minutes until the aromas are released.

Return lamb to wok and add kaffir lime leaves, satay sauce, cinnamon, coconut milk, water and fish sauce and simmer, covered, for 30 minutes or until meat is almost tender.

Add the sweet potato and cook, uncovered, for a further 15 minutes, stirring occasionally, until the sweet potato is soft.

Serve on a bed of rice topped with coriander and toasted peanuts or almonds.

Ainsley Aitcheson, Wellington Point

THARNTIP'S THAI BASIL AND GARLIC PRAWN STIR-FRY

Thai food has the culinary feature of combining different tastes to create a unique dish – usually with one or two 'leading' tastes and up to three 'support' tastes. A dish may have a spicy leading taste, but be sweet, sour and bitter as well. Tharntip's Thai Basil and Garlic Prawn Stir-Fry has a sweet and spicy leading taste, which is complemented by the tang of basil and slight sourness of the tomato. Serve with fragrant jasmine white rice.

400g large green prawns, peeled
3 tablespoons vegetable oil
2–3 garlic cloves, crushed
100g bamboo shoots, chopped
2 medium-sized red chillies, medium hot, de-seeded and diced
2 large tomatoes, sliced
½ teaspoon sugar
1½ tablespoons basil, roughly chopped
½ tablespoon fish sauce
1 tablespoon soy sauce
1 tablespoon of sweet soy sauce

Clean and de-vein prawns, cutting in half lengthwise, but don't cut right through, so the prawns are butterflied.

Heat oil in a wok and add garlic followed by the prawns. Stir-fry until the prawns just start to change colour. Add bamboo shoots, chillies, tomatoes, sugar and soy and fish sauces and stir-fry for a couple of minutes. Lastly, add the basil and stir through.

Serve immediately.

Note: Chicken can be substituted for the prawns.

Ken and Tharntip Bennett, Cornubia

TWO COURSES – ONE POT

We find this to be a really simple way to provide a two-course meal for the family. The preparation is minimal and both entree and main course virtually cook themselves, allowing plenty of time for good old-fashioned conversation – a dying commodity!

3–4 tablespoons of olive oil
1 medium onion, finely chopped
3–4 cloves garlic, crushed
750g corner cut topside beef
3 tablespoons tomato paste
800g tin peeled tomatoes
1 dessertspoon dried thyme
1 tablespoon dried oregano
1 tablespoon dried basil
300ml (1¼ cups) dry red wine
freshly ground black pepper
500g spaghetti
2 tablespoons chopped parsley
2 tablespoons finely grated Parmesan

Heat the olive oil in either a flameproof casserole or a thick-bottomed pan with a lid. Gently cook the onion and garlic until onion softens, about 3 minutes. Remove to a small bowl.

Brown the meat on high heat. Return the onions and garlic to the pan with the tomato paste and cook for 1 minute. Add the tomatoes with all their juice, the herbs and wine and bring to the boil. Reduce the heat to the lowest setting and cook, covered, for between 2 and 2½ hours, stirring occasionally to ensure the tomatoes are broken up.

When cooked, season with freshly ground pepper.

Cook spaghetti in a large pot of boiling salted water, drain and mix in sufficient of the meat sauce to give the pasta a liberal coating. Garnish with chopped parsley and serve as an entree with grated Parmesan.

Remove topside from the sauce and serve thick slices with additional sauce on the side.

This is best accompanied by jacket potato and a lightly dressed green salad.

Note: This dish can also be cooked in a low (160°C) oven.

Eddie Vann, Maleny

Vegetarian Lasagne

4 zucchini, sliced lengthways
3 tablespoons olive oil
2 cloves garlic, crushed
salt and pepper
1 cup tomato passata
1 packet instant lasagne sheets
150g baby spinach, steamed for 2 minutes
2 bunches asparagus, steamed 3 minutes
200g feta cheese
4 tomatoes, sliced thinly
1 tablespoon dried oregano
1 cup breadcrumbs

Preheat oven 200°C.

Place zucchini on baking tray, drizzle with olive oil and scatter with garlic, salt and pepper and bake until golden.

Spread half the passata evenly over the base of a lasagne dish. Place a single layer of lasagne sheets on top of the passata then top with zucchini, spinach, asparagus and feta cheese and season with salt and pepper. Cover with another layer of lasagne sheets then pour over the remaining tomato passata.

Arrange tomato slices over the passata and sprinkle with the oregano and breadcrumbs. Drizzle with olive oil from the zucchini tray. Bake for 40–45 minutes, or until lasagne is cooked through.

Keiran Darby, Jindalee

VIETNAMESE CHICKEN AND MINT SALAD

2 skinless chicken breasts
500g (5 cups) bean sprouts
155g (1 cup) grated carrot
½ cup freshly chopped mint leaves
fresh coriander leaves for garnish
crisp-fried shallots or fried peanuts for garnish

DRESSING
2 fresh chillies, seeded and finely chopped
3 cloves garlic, finely chopped
2 tablespoons palm sugar
1 tablespoon rice vinegar
4 tablespoons fresh lime juice
4 tablespoons fish sauce
3 tablespoons peanut oil
2 spring onions

For the dressing, combine all ingredients and leave for 30 minutes to allow the flavours to develop.

Place chicken breasts in gently simmering water or stock for about 8 minutes. When firm to touch, remove and allow to cool before slicing finely.

Toss chicken through vegetables and mint and moisten with dressing. Arrange on a platter and garnish with coriander. Sprinkle with crisp-fried shallots or peanuts, if desired.

Anna Bligh, Queensland Premier

SIDE DISHES

BARBECUE BEANS

The credit for this should go to my mum, Kay. Where she got it I don't know but it has been a popular dish in our house for as long as I can remember. It is a great side meal for any barbecue and I have taken it to many parties as an alternative to salad – it never lasts long. It can be made well in advance, keeps well in the fridge, can be reheated, and is good as leftovers on toast. I really can't see anything bad about it for you. I can make it well but, like all things, it tastes better when Mum does it.

2 tablespoons butter
2 large onions, chopped
1 clove garlic, crushed
400g bacon, chopped
400g tin tomato soup
125ml (½ cup) water
1 teaspoon white vinegar
2 teaspoons brown sugar
2 teaspoons Worcestershire sauce
½ teaspoon dry mustard
2 x 400g cans of four bean mix, rinsed and drained

Heat butter in a large heavy based saucepan and add onion, garlic and bacon and sauté until onion is soft. Add tomato soup and stir through.

Combine water, vinegar, brown sugar, Worcestershire sauce and mustard and simmer for 10 minutes, stirring occasionally. Add beans and cook a further 3 minutes.

Martin Hayes, Tewantin

BOILED SALAD DRESSING

This was my mother's recipe, and I use it all the time since she passed away.

2 eggs
230g (1 cup) caster sugar
2 teaspoons plain flour
2 teaspoons salt
2 teaspoons mustard
250ml (1 cup) milk
250ml (1 cup) white vinegar

Beat together eggs and sugar until sugar is dissolved. Mix flour, salt and mustard with the milk and add to the egg mixture. Place in a saucepan and stir over low heat, adding vinegar as the mixture starts to warm. Stir constantly until the mixture thickens and coats the back of a spoon.

Pour into sterilised jars and keep refrigerated. The dressing will thicken when cool.

Jillian Hollis, Caboolture

CAPSICUMS WITH HALOUMI, CHILLI AND PINE NUTS

3 red capsicums, halved
salt and pepper
2 tablespoons olive oil
250g haloumi cheese, cut into 6 slices

DRESSING
juice of 1 lemon
1 garlic clove, crushed
1 red chilli, finely chopped
2 tablespoons pine nuts, toasted
small bunch parsley, chopped
3 tablespoons olive oil, plus extra for drizzling

Preheat the oven to 200°C. Put the capsicums on a baking tray in a single layer. Season with salt and pepper and drizzle with olive oil. Bake for 10–15 minutes until softened. Place a piece of haloumi inside each capsicum half and grill until the cheese is golden.

Place all dressing ingredients in a mixing bowl and whisk to combine.

To serve, place the peppers on a serving plate and drizzle with the dressing.

Keiran Darby, Jindalee

EFRAT'S COUSCOUS SALAD

This very easy couscous salad does not need to be pre-soaked as there is enough liquid in the ingredients to moisten the couscous.

280g (1½ cups) couscous
440g tin diced tomatoes
1 onion, finely diced
½ cup chopped mint
80–125ml (⅓–½ cup) lemon juice
60ml (¼ cup) olive oil
salt
freshly ground black pepper
¼ cup finely chopped parsley

Combine all ingredients in a mixing bowl. Taste and adjust with salt and lemon juice to your liking. Cover the salad and refrigerate overnight, stirring occasionally.

Serve with meat or fish, or just enjoy on its own.

Jan Rhoades, Upper Mt Gravatt

KEN'S QUEENSLAND PICO DE GALLO

Having a childhood in a primarily Spanish-speaking neighbourhood in Los Angeles, the food of Mexico was a normal daily dining event – both at school and at home. This dish combines the flavours of my childhood with the taste of my home for the last 20 years, Queensland.

Queensland Pico de Gallo is a refreshing and easily prepared dish enjoyed either as a dip for corn chips, added to a wrap or tortilla, or as a condiment for meat or fish. This dish is served cold and can be prepared the day before, but best 1–2 hours before serving. Pico de Gallo can be stored for up to 4 days in the refrigerator.

4 large ripe tomatoes
1 large Spanish (red) onion
1 bunch coriander
3–4 tablespoons lime juice
pulp of 1 large passionfruit
salt and pepper

Dice tomatoes and onions and combine in a bowl. Chop the coriander and add to the tomato mixture with the lime juice, passionfruit pulp and salt and pepper. Stir gently to mix.

Taste and adjust flavour with seasoning or lime juice as desired.

Ken and Tharntip Bennett, Cornubia

MACADAMIA AND CORIANDER PESTO

This pesto is good mixed through pasta or spread on crackers.

1 bunch coriander, well washed
4 cloves garlic
60g (½ cup) macadamias
60g (⅔ cup) romano or Parmesan cheese, grated
125ml (½ cup) olive oil

Place coriander leaves, stalks and roots, garlic, macadamias and cheese in a food processor or blender and process until finely chopped.

With machine running, slowly pour in the oil, scraping down the sides of the bowl a few times, until the mixture reaches a spreading consistency, adding more oil if necessary.

Refrigerate for at least 1 hour before using to allow the flavours to develop.

Wendy Wright, East Toowoomba

POTATO SALAD

This recipe was given to me by my good friend, the late Bernard King; it is his special potato salad which I – and those who have tasted it – love.

10–12 small white potatoes, cut in half
4 large eggs, hard boiled, cooled and peeled
125g (½ cup) sour cream
4 tablespoons good mayonnaise
3 tablespoons chopped flat leaf parsley
black pepper

Boil potatoes until just soft; allow to cool then place in a serving bowl. Roughly chop the eggs and add to the potatoes.

Mix the sour cream and mayonnaise in a separate dish until well combined. Add to potatoes with the parsley and gently combine until the dressing evenly coats the potato mixture. Grind pepper lightly on the top of salad.

Cover and cool in refrigerator until ready to serve.

Judith Ferber, Gold Coast

SPICED ALMONDS

1¼ tablespoons peanut oil
1 tablespoon caster sugar
465g (3 cups) blanched whole almonds
5 teaspoons caster sugar, extra
2 teaspoons salt
2 teaspoons ground cumin
1⅓ teaspoons dried chilli flakes

Heat oil in a heavy frying pan. Add 1 tablespoon of the sugar and stir until sugar has melted. Add almonds and stir until they turn golden.

Remove from the heat with a slotted spoon to a mixing bowl and mix with remaining ingredients. Allow nuts to cool before storing in an airtight container.

Mary Dickinson, Yeronga

DESSERTS

APPLE CRUMBLE

2 teaspoons butter
5 Granny Smith apples, peeled, cored and sliced
115g (½ cup) sugar
150g (1 cup) plain flour
1 tablespoon brown sugar
1½ teaspoons ground ginger
1 teaspoon baking powder
60g (¼ cup) butter, extra, cut into small cubes

Preheat oven to 180°C.

Gently melt butter in medium-sized saucepan but do not allow it to brown. Add apples and sugar and cook over gentle heat, covered, until slightly soft. Remove from the heat and allow to cool slightly.

Rub together flour, brown sugar, ginger, baking powder and extra butter until mixture resemble breadcrumbs. Spoon apples into ovenproof dish and cover with crumble mixture.

Bake for 40 minutes or until topping is browned and bubbling at edges.

Robyn Foster, Mount Cotton

APPLE, RHUBARB AND MULBERRY PIE

The berries come from my sister's trees in suburban Brisbane and every mouthful reminds me of how grateful I am to have such a wonderful sister.

2 cups peeled and diced apples
250g (2 cups) diced rhubarb
250g (2 cups) mulberries
220g (⅔ cup) sugar
85ml (⅓ cup) apple cider
1 teaspoon vanilla paste
3 tablespoons cornflour
60ml (¼ cup) lemon juice
30g (¼ cup) plain flour
45g (¼ cup) brown sugar
25g (¼ cup) rolled oats
25g (¼ cup) desiccated coconut
3 tablespoons butter
1 prepared pie crust, bought or homemade

Preheat the oven to 210°C.

Place the apples, rhubarb, mulberries, sugar, apple cider and vanilla paste in a large saucepan and cook over medium heat, stirring occasionally, until the apples and rhubarb start to soften. Combine the cornflour and lemon juice in a small bowl, add to the fruit mixture and stir over heat until mixture has thickened.

Combine plain flour, brown sugar, rolled oats and coconut in a mixing bowl and rub in the butter. Spoon fruit filling into the pastry shell and sprinkle over the crumble topping.

Bake for 30–40 minutes or until the top is golden.

Sue Ruming, Alexandra Headland

ALMOND AND APRICOT TART

PASTRY
150g (1 cup) flour
½ teaspoon baking powder
pinch salt
60g (¼ cup) butter
1 tablespoon sugar
1 small egg yolk, mixed with a little cold water

FILLING
60g (¼ cup) butter
2 tablespoons caster sugar
1 egg
25g (¼ cup) ground almonds
3½ crushed sweet biscuits
½ teaspoon almond essence
2 tablespoons apricot jam

2 tablespoons icing sugar

Preheat oven to 180°C.

Sift flour, baking powder and salt together and rub in butter. Add sugar and blend to a firm dough with egg yolk.

Roll pastry out on floured surface to 1cm thick and press into a 20cm sandwich cake tin.

For the filling, cream butter and sugar until light and fluffy. Separate egg and add yolk to butter mixture. Beat to combine. Add ground almonds, crushed biscuits and almond essence and mix well. Beat egg white until stiff peaks form and fold into almond mixture.

Spread jam over pastry base then top with almond mixture. Cut left over pastry into thin strips and create a crisscross pattern on top of the pie.

Bake for 25–30 minutes.

Combine icing sugar with a little water to a spreadable consistency. When the pie is cold, brush the icing over top and allow to set.

Beverley McNaughton, Brighton

DARK CHOCOLATE MOUSSE

This was my mother's favourite recipe to make for me when I had been a good girl. Unlike most chocolate mousse recipes, this one does not include cream.

170g dark chocolate
80ml (⅓ cup) milk
1 egg yolk
4 egg whites
1 tablespoon caster sugar

Melt chocolate in the microwave or in a bowl set over a saucepan of simmering water. Bring milk to the boil and pour over melted chocolate, whisking to combine. Add egg yolk and whisk again. Set aside to cool.

Beat egg whites to firm peaks, gradually adding sugar. Add one-third of the egg whites to the chocolate mixture and mix gently. Add the remaining egg whites and fold through lightly to combine.

Chill well before serving.

Barbara Noble, North Tamborine

EASY AS APPLE PIE

A never-fail recipe. So simple to make, its preparation time is approximately 10 minutes. Back in the 1970s a work colleague brought this as her contribution to a shared lunch. I have been making it ever since.

210g (1½ cups) plain flour
170g (¾ cup) sugar
1 teaspoon vanilla essence
1 egg
125g (½ cup) butter, melted
800g tinned pie fruit or equivalent of stewed fruit
1 teaspoon sugar
½ teaspoon ground cinnamon

Preheat oven to 190°C.

Mix together flour, sugar, vanilla, egg and butter to form a soft dough. Press three-quarters of the pastry into a base of a large pie dish. Fill with tinned or stewed fruit.

Crumble over the remaining pastry and sprinkle the sugar and cinnamon on top.

Bake for 50–55 minutes.

Serve warm or cold with custard, cream or ice cream.

Collein Avery, Newport

FEEL-GOOD CHOCOLATE MOUSSE

This is my favourite recipe and is close to my heart because I use it to cheer up my friends whenever they're having a hard day. It's spirit lifting, and the perfect feel-good food.

300g dark chocolate
3 eggs, lightly beaten
80g (⅓ cup) caster sugar
1 teaspoon cocoa powder
350ml (1⅓ cups) cream

Melt the chocolate in the microwave, or in a bowl set over a saucepan of simmering water, stirring often, then set aside to cool.

Beat the eggs and sugar in a large mixing bowl until pale and the mixture has about doubled in size. Fold the melted chocolate into the egg mixture with a large spoon until combined. Sift the cocoa powder over the chocolate mixture and fold in.

Beat the cream in another bowl until soft peaks form. Carefully fold the cream into the chocolate mixture until combined and smooth.

Spoon mousse into 6 (150–200ml) glasses and leave in the refrigerator to set for at least an hour, but preferably 2–3 hours.

Maggie McDonald, Surfers Paradise

GOLDEN SYRUP DUMPLINGS

This recipe was given to me by my daughter, Nicky, and has been a family favourite for many years. I always prepare this dish for when my sons come to visit – it is their favourite dessert.

180g (1¼ cup) self-raising flour
1½ tablespoons butter
60ml (¼ cup) golden syrup
80ml (⅓ cup) milk
1½ tablespoons butter, extra
95g (½ cup, lightly packed) brown sugar
125ml (½ cup) golden syrup, extra
375ml (1½ cups) water
2 teaspoons grated lemon rind

Sift flour into basin and rub in butter. Combine syrup and milk. Make a well in the centre of dry ingredients and gradually stir in milk mixture until ingredients are combined. Do not overbeat. Mixture should be moist and sticky.

Make sauce by combining extra butter, brown sugar, syrup, water and lemon rind in a heatproof dish. Cover dish with plastic wrap and microwave on full power for 6 minutes, stirring occasionally to dissolve the sugar.

With floured hands, roll the dumpling mixture into walnut-sized balls. Place into boiling syrup. Cover the dish loosely with plastic wrap. Microwave on full power for 3–4 minutes or until dumplings are well risen and firm.

Serve immediately.

Pat Cannard, Murrumba Downs

IVY MARTIN'S STEAMED PUDDING

This recipe was given to me by a friend and neighbour some 40 years ago. Ivy is now deceased but I would like this recipe to be published in her memory.

2 tablespoons golden syrup
185ml (¾ cup) milk
¼ teaspoon bicarbonate of soda
2 tablespoons golden syrup, extra
2 tablespoons butter or margarine
180g (1¼ cups) self-raising flour

Lightly grease a pudding steamer and pour the golden syrup into the base.

Combine milk and bicarbonate of soda in a small saucepan. Add extra golden syrup and butter and heat until the butter has melted. Remove from the heat and stir in the flour.

Spoon mixture into the steamer and seal with the lid.

Place steamer into a saucepan and add boiling water to come halfway up the sides of the steamer. Cover the saucepan and maintain the water at a simmer for 20 minutes.

Serve immediately.

Deirdre Graham, Stafford

JAM ROLY POLY

Pastry

180g (1¼ cups) self-raising flour
1 teaspoon caster sugar
3 tablespoons butter
2 tablespoons milk, for mixing
160g (½ cup) raspberry jam

Syrup

310ml (1¼ cups) boiling water
2 tablespoons butter
1 tablespoon sugar

Preheat oven to 180°C.

Combine sifted flour with caster sugar in a mixing bowl and rub in butter with fingertips until the mixture resembles breadcrumbs. Make a well in the centre of the mixture and add milk, mixing with a blunt knife, to form a firm dough. Add more milk if dough is too stiff.

Turn dough out onto a lightly floured surface and gently form into a ball. Roll out dough to form a rectangular shape approximately 1cm thick and spread with the jam, stopping 4cm of the edge. Roll up pastry from longest edge and pinch in ends. Place seam down in a horseshoe shape inside a greased baking dish.

Combine all the syrup ingredients in a small bowl and stir until the sugar has dissolved then pour over the roly poly. Bake for 25 minutes.

Serve hot with whipped cream or warm custard.

Debbie Vincent, Loganholme

LEMON DELICIOUS

2 tablespoons butter
170g (¾ cup) caster sugar
4 tablespoons self-raising flour
pinch salt
2 eggs, separated
finely grated zest of 1 lemon
strained juice of 2 lemons
250ml (1 cup) milk

Preheat oven to 180°C. Lightly grease a 1½-litre (6-cup) ovenproof dish.

Cream butter and sugar until light and fluffy. Add sifted flour, salt, egg yolks, lemon zest and juice and mix. Stir in the milk.

Beat egg whites to stiff peaks and fold into the creamed mixture. Pour into dish then place dish in a large pan and fill pan with hot water to halfway up the pudding dish.

Bake for 35–40 minutes or until light golden on top.

Note: To test if pudding is cooked, dip a knife into the centre and if it comes out clean it is cooked. If the blade has mixture on it, cook a further 5–10 minutes.

Yvonne Rimmer, New Farm

MAGPIE PUDDING

This self-saucing dark and white chocolate pudding is certain to cheer you as do the magpies in your garden after the rain.

150g (1 cup) self-raising flour
2 tablespoons cocoa powder
90g (⅓ cup) butter, melted
125ml (½ cup) milk
1 teaspoon vanilla essence
115g (½ cup) caster sugar
1 dessertspoon instant coffee granules
75g (½ cup) chopped white chocolate
115g (½ cup) brown sugar
1 tablespoon cocoa powder, extra
375ml (1½ cups) boiling water

Preheat oven to 180°C. Grease a 1½-litre (6-cup) ovenproof dish.

Sift together the flour and cocoa powder. Combine butter, milk, vanilla, sugar, coffee granules and white chocolate in a mixing bowl. Spoon mixture into dish. Sprinkle the top with brown sugar and extra cocoa powder. Gently pour over the boiling water and place dish on an oven tray.

Bake for about 40–45 minutes or until the top is firm. Cover loosely with foil if the top is becoming too brown.

Serve warm, dusted with icing sugar.

Sonia Benesovsky, Nambour

MEG'S CHRISTMAS PUDDING

*My mother was a superb cook and when she passed away
some 10 years ago, I realised that my siblings and I
couldn't share her cookbook. This book is an old leather
hide journal which Mom acquired during our time in
Africa, and throughout her life she recorded recipes of
note, who gave them to her, and then added her own touch
over time. The journal is stained and the pages well worn,
but a loved treasure. My father has learnt to cook from it
and, some years ago, I borrowed the journal, typed it all
out and had it bound into a hardcover cookbook titled*
From Meg's Kitchen *for each of my siblings. I copied the
recipes verbatim from her book, but have always suspected
that Mom enjoyed a wine or two while cooking and did
not feel the need to record each step in detail.*

*This pudding can be made three months before
Christmas and stored in a cool, dark pantry.*

375g (1½ cups) butter
250g (1 cup, firmly packed) brown sugar
4 eggs, lightly beaten
250g (3¼ cups) white breadcrumbs
500g (4 cups) raisins
500g (4 cups) sultanas
125g (1 cup) currants
250g (1½ cups) dates, chopped
95g (½ cup) mixed peel
250g (1¾ cups) plain flour
¼ teaspoon salt
1 tablespoon mixed spice
2 teaspoons ground nutmeg
½ teaspoon bicarbonate of soda
250ml (1 cup) brandy

Beat butter and sugar until light and creamy. Add eggs and beat again.

Stir in remaining ingredients and mix well.

Butter a large pudding bowl and line the base with baking paper. Spoon pudding mixture into the bowl and smooth the top. Cover pudding with a layer of baking paper and a layer of foil and tie firmly with string. Place bowl into a large boiling pot and fill with boiling water to come two-thirds of the way up the side of the bowl. Maintain water at a simmer and steam the pudding for 6–7 hours. Replenish boiling water as needed.

Remove pudding from the pot and allow to cool before storing in a cool, dark, dry place.

When ready to serve, steam the pudding in the same way as above for 2 hours.

Kirsten Dyer, Ashgrove

MUM'S EASY PAVLOVA

Afternoon tea time around the kitchen table in Dalby sometimes resembled a footy scrum, especially if it was Mum's Easy Pavlova on offer. There were five of us kids, all fighting for the biggest slice, and it would disappear in no time!

1 teaspoon cornflour
2 egg whites
350g (1½ cups) caster sugar
½ teaspoon vanilla
1 teaspoon vinegar
4 tablespoons boiling water

Preheat oven to 180°C. Grease a baking tray and lightly dust with cornflour then shake off the excess.

Put all ingredients in the small bowl of an electric mixer. Beat at high speed till the mixture is very thick; this will take about 15 minutes. Scrape mixture onto a baking sheet, building it up around the sides.

For a large pavlova, bake in 180°C oven for 10 minutes then reduce the heat to 150°C and bake for another 45 minutes. Allow pavlova to cool in the oven.

For individual pavlovas, bake for 10 minutes at 180°C and then 30 minutes at 150°C.

Fill pavlova with whipped cream, passionfruit and strawberries.

Note: You can make small individual pavlovas with this mixture or one large 23–28cm one. Other fruit can be used such as mangoes, kiwifruit or sliced peaches.

Madonna King, 612 ABC Brisbane Mornings presenter

THE NEXT BEST THING TO ROBERT REDFORD

This is my and my friend's number one favourite. It is an adaptation of a recipe passed onto me in New Guinea by a friend. 'Will you please bring "Robert Redford"?' is a constant request for pot lucks and dinner parties.

BASE
90g (⅓ cup) butter, melted
250g packet shortbread biscuits, crushed

FIRST LAYER
250g cream cheese
300ml cream
3 tablespoon icing sugar
1 teaspoon vanilla essence

SECOND LAYER
185g (¾ cup) butter
185g (1½ cups) icing sugar
90g (¾ cup) cocoa powder
2 teaspoons vanilla essence
3 eggs

THIRD LAYER
300ml cream
30g (¼ cup) icing sugar
2 teaspoons vanilla essence

100g dark chocolate
60g (½ cup) chopped walnuts

Line a 22cm x 30cm tin with baking paper.

Combine butter and biscuit crumbs and press into the tin.

For the first layer, beat together cream cheese and cream, then sift over icing sugar. Add vanilla and beat until smooth. Pour over the biscuit base.

For the second layer, cream sugar until light and fluffy. Sift over icing sugar and cocoa then add eggs and vanilla. Beat until smooth. Pour over the first layer.

For the third layer, combine all ingredients in a mixing bowl and beat until smooth. Pour over second layer.

Finely grate the chocolate and sprinkle over the top. Finish with a layer of walnuts.

Chill the cheesecake in the refrigerator for at least 4 hours.

Note: 1 teaspoon vanilla essence and 2 tablespoons brandy can be used instead of 2 teaspoons vanilla essence.

Jo Belfield, Bellbowrie

NO-FUSS ICE CREAM

This recipe is a family favourite for birthdays and a summer holiday treat. It does not require any special equipment.

600ml (2⅓ cups) cream
1 tablespoon lemon juice
5 tablespoons brown sugar
2 tablespoons cocoa

Place all ingredients in a large bowl and beat with electric mixer until soft peaks have formed.

Pour into sealable, freezer-safe container (old ice cream containers work well), cover and freeze overnight.

To serve, allow to soften for 5 minutes on bench top before scooping out.

Note: Many other flavours can be used instead of the cocoa, such as 1 teaspoon vanilla essence or 1 mashed ripe banana or pieces of biscuit or chocolate.

Violet De Groot, Woodhill

Passionfruit Tart

Pastry
2 tablespoons butter
2 tablespoons sugar
1 egg
150g (1 cup) self-raising flour
60g (½ cup) custard powder

Filling
250ml (1 cup) milk
115g (½ cup) sugar
1 dessertspoon butter
2 tablespoons cornflour
1 egg
juice of ½ lemon
pulp of 2–3 passionfruit

Preheat oven to 180°C.

Cream together the butter and sugar until light and fluffy. Mix through egg, flour and custard powder. Press pastry into a pie dish and bake for 10–15 minutes or until crisp.

For the filling, place milk, sugar and butter in a saucepan and bring to the boil.

Add cornflour, stirring constantly, and remove from heat when the mixture has thickened. Combine egg, lemon and passionfruit and beat into the milk mixture. Set aside to cool then pour into tart shell.

Serve cold.

Margaret Crevola, Wishart

STICKY DATE PUDDING

PUDDING
250g (1½ cups) dates, chopped
375ml (1½ cups) water
½ teaspoon bicarbonate of soda
1 tablespoon olive or vegetable oil
2 eggs
115g (½ cup, firmly packed) brown sugar
2 teaspoons vanilla extract
125ml (½ cup) milk
225g (1¾ cups) self-raising flour

TOFFEE SAUCE
200g butter, chopped
250ml (1 cup) pouring cream
385g (1⅔ cups, firmly packed) brown sugar

Preheat the oven to 180°C. Grease a 23cm cake tin and line with baking paper.

Combine dates and water in a saucepan and simmer for 10 minutes or until the dates are soft, then remove from heat and stir in the bicarbonate of soda. Allow to cool then stir in the oil.

Beat the eggs, sugar and vanilla in a bowl until creamy. Add the milk, flour and date mixture and mix well. Pour into cake tin and bake for 35 minutes or until a skewer inserted into the centre of the cake comes out clean.

For the toffee sauce, place the butter, cream and sugar in a saucepan over a low heat and stir until the sugar is dissolved. Increase the heat and simmer for 5 minutes or until the sauce is thick.

To serve, cut pudding into thick slices and serve with warm toffee sauce.

Nora Martin, Allambie Heights

TEA-TIME TREATS

ALMOND STARS

My great aunt and I used to bake these biscuits for Christmas when I was a little girl back in Germany. We had a very special relationship and I lived with her for a while when I went to kindy. When I moved out, I asked my aunt for the recipe. She gave it to me and I've made these biscuits every Christmas since, except for the first year I moved to Australia 10 years ago. They are still my all-time favourite Christmas biscuits and they always remind me of my childhood and the love my very special aunt had for me.

250g (1¾ cups) plain flour
150g (⅔ cup) white sugar
70g (⅔ cup) ground almonds
1 pinch cinnamon
200g unsalted butter
2 egg yolks
½ teaspoon vanilla bean paste
1 egg yolk, extra
1 dessertspoon milk
230g (1½ cups) blanched almonds

Preheat oven to 180°C.

Combine flour, sugar, ground almonds and cinnamon in a bowl. Rub in the butter until mixture resembles breadcrumbs. Beat eggs and vanilla together then add to the butter mixture and mix to a dough. Wrap in plastic and refrigerate for an hour.

Line a baking tray with baking paper. Roll out the dough on a floured surface to a thickness of 7mm. Cut out shapes using a star cutter and place them on the baking tray.

Beat the extra egg yolk with the milk and brush this mixture on the top of stars. Press an almond into the centre of each star and bake for 10 minutes or until golden brown. Remove from the oven and cool on a wire rack.

Uli Esser, Upper Kedron

BIG BATCH BIKKIES

This recipe is quick, easy and totally versatile. It can be made from what you have in the cupboard and will make up to 5 dozen biscuits.

500g butter, softened
750g (5 cups) plain flour
230g (1 cup) caster sugar
440g tin condensed milk

Preheat oven to 170°C. Line baking trays with baking paper.

Place all ingredients in an electric mixer and combine with the dough hook. Roll tablespoonfuls of the mixture into balls and place on a tray. Flatten the balls with a fork and bake for 15 minutes.

Remove from the oven and rest on the trays for a few minutes before placing on a wire rack to cool completely.

Note: Chocolate chips, chocolate buttons, dried fruit or nuts can be added to the mixture.

Kerrie Wells, Fairfield

CHOC-CHERRY SCONES

This is our family favourite. They are so easy to make and never fail. They taste like a cross between a cake and a cookie. Our kitchen smells of choc-cherry bliss so we thought we would like other people's kitchens to smell so good too.

1 egg
150ml (⅔ cup) milk
150ml (⅔ cup) cream
450g (3 cups) self-raising flour
40g (⅓ cup) cocoa powder
80g (⅓ cup) caster sugar
100g (⅓ cup) glace cherries, chopped
100g (⅔ cup) chocolate buttons, chopped
1 tablespoon milk
1 tablespoon caster sugar, extra

Preheat oven to 200°C. Line a baking tray with baking paper.

Whisk together egg, milk and cream in a small bowl. Combine the remaining ingredients in a large mixing bowl. Add wet ingredients to dry ingredients, mixing with a blunt knife.

Turn dough out onto a floured surface and knead lightly. Pat dough into a round 2cm high and cut out scones using a scone cutter and place on tray. Brush scones with milk and sprinkle with sugar.

Bake for 10–15 minutes. Remove from the oven and serve with cream.

Jacqui Cawthan, Highland Park

CHOC-PEANUT BISCUITS

These bikkies have been enjoyed by my family for over 50 years. The original recipe was from my grandmother.

125g (½ cup) butter
125g (½ cup) sugar
1 egg, lightly beaten
90g (¾ cup) plain flour
1 tablespoon cocoa powder
1 teaspoon baking powder
½ teaspoon salt
250g (1½ cups) raw peanuts

Preheat oven to 180°C. Line a baking tray with baking paper.

Cream butter and sugar then add egg and beat well. Sift together the flour, cocoa powder, baking powder and salt and fold into the creamed butter and sugar. Lastly stir in the peanuts.

If the mixture is too dry, add a little milk and stir in well. Place teaspoonfuls onto the tray and bake for about 20 minutes or until golden. Remove from the oven and cool biscuits on a wire rack.

Store in an airtight container.

Note: Be careful not to overcook the biscuits as the peanuts have a tendency to burn.

Kathy Mitchell, Varsity Lakes

CHOCOLATE AND MACADAMIA BISCUITS

150g (⅔ cup) butter
200g (1 cup, firmly packed) brown sugar
1 egg
1 egg yolk
225g (1⅔ cups) plain flour
1 teaspoon baking powder
pinch bicarbonate of soda
pinch of salt
100g (¾ cup) roughly chopped macadamias
200g (1⅓ cups) roughly chopped dark chocolate

Preheat oven to 180°C. Line a baking tray with baking paper.

Cream the butter and sugar until light and fluffy. Beat in egg and egg yolk. Sift together the flour, baking powder, bicarbonate of soda and salt and stir into the creamed mixture. Lastly, stir in the macadamias and chocolate.

Tip dough onto baking paper and form into a log 3–4cm in diameter, roll up tightly in the paper and refrigerate for 2 hours.

When ready to bake, slice log into 1cm wide discs and place on baking tray. Bake for 14 minutes. Remove from the oven and cool on wire rack.

Note: You can divide the dough into 2 logs and keep one in the freezer for later.

Kathy Kovago, Castaways Beach

CHOCOLATE ROUGHS

This is my grandmother's recipe of unknown origin. My mother remembers them being made in the 1930s and she has been making them for our family since I can remember.

125g (½ cup) butter
115g (½ cup) caster sugar
1 egg
150g (1 cup) self-raising flour
2 generous tablespoons cocoa powder
135g (1½ cups) desiccated coconut

Preheat oven to 180°C. Line a baking tray with baking paper.

Cream the butter and sugar then add the egg and beat well. Sift together the flour and cocoa powder and fold into creamed mixture with the coconut.

Place teaspoonfuls of mixture on the baking tray and bake for 15 minutes.

Note: The Coconut Roughs can be joined with chocolate icing if desired.

Jane Powell, Taringa

COFFEE VENETIAN BISCUITS

A lovely buttery biscuit and a favourite with all.

125g (½ cup) butter
125g (½ cup) caster sugar
1 egg yolk
1 tablespoon coffee essence
180g (1¼ cups) plain flour
1 teaspoon cream of tartar
½ teaspoon bicarbonate of soda
blanched almonds
extra caster sugar

Preheat oven to 180°C. Line a baking tray with baking paper.

Cream the butter and sugar until light and fluffy, add egg yolk and coffee essence and beat again. Stir in sifted dry ingredients and mix until a smooth dough forms.

Roll into small balls, toss in caster sugar and place on the baking tray. Press a blanched almond on top and bake in the oven for 15 minutes or until golden.

Jillian Hollis, Caboolture

EILEEN'S CUSTARD CREAM BISCUITS

This recipe was given to me by a wonderful friend in her late 80s, who was born and bred on the Sunshine Coast. Not only is she a wonderful woman who has given so much of her time to community service, but she has seen her fair share of famine and flood.

160g (⅔ cup) butter
60g (½ cup) icing sugar
210g (1½ cups) plain flour
pinch salt
60g (½ cup) custard powder

ICING
185g (1½ cups) sifted icing sugar
1 dessertspoon butter, softened
juice of ¼ lemon

Preheat oven to 170°C. Grease a baking tray.

Cream butter and icing sugar. Sift flour, salt and custard powder together and gradually add to butter and sugar, stirring to make a soft paste.

Roll dessertspoonfuls of the mixture into small balls and place on the tray. Press each biscuit down slightly with a floured fork and bake in the oven for about 12 minutes or until a pale golden colour.

For the icing, place ingredients in a small bowl and beat until smooth. Taste and add more lemon juice if desired.

Spread the base of one biscuit with lemon icing and top with another biscuit.

Nicola Booth, Woodford

Everybody's Favourite Biscuits

This recipe is so versatile and can be made with different nuts, chocolate pieces, citrus zest, or sandwiched together with icing – it's up to your imagination.

125g (½ cup) butter
60g (½ cup) icing sugar
1 teaspoon vanilla essence
pinch salt
150g (1 cup) self-raising flour
1 dessertspoon custard powder
½ cup finely chopped almonds

Preheat oven to 180°C. Grease a baking tray.

Cream the butter, sugar, vanilla and salt until light and fluffy. Sift together the flour and custard powder and stir into the creamed mixture with the almonds.

Place teaspoonfuls of mixture on the tray, allowing room to spread, and bake for 16 minutes. Remove from the oven and rest on the tray for 3 minutes before placing on a wire rack to cool.

Vickie McEnery, Veteran

FRUITY CORNFLAKE BISCUITS

150g (5 cups) cornflakes
90g (1 cup) desiccated coconut
115g (½ cup) firmly packed, brown sugar
60g (1 cup) sultanas
160g (1 cup) dates, chopped
150g (1 cup) self-raising flour
185g (¾ cup) butter, melted
2 eggs, lightly beaten

Preheat oven to 180°C. Lightly grease a baking tray.

Combine cornflakes, coconut, sugar, sultanas, dates and flour in a large mixing bowl. Add butter and eggs and mix well.

Shape heaped tablespoons of mixture into balls and place about 5cm apart on trays. Flatten slightly with a fork. Bake in the oven for 10 minutes or until golden brown.

Remove from the oven and leave biscuits on the tray for 5 minutes before cooling on a wire rack.

Marian Beeston, Waterford

GEOFF'S FAMOUS CHOCOLATE FUDGE BROWNIES

This recipe belongs to Geoff, who recently passed away. Geoff was a tireless worker for many charities and whenever there was a morning tea, Geoff supplied his 'famous' brownies. They gained such a reputation that this recipe was printed on the back of the order of service at his funeral.

185g (1¼ cups) dark chocolate
125g (½ cup) butter
170g (¾ cup) caster sugar
2 eggs
150g (1 cup) plain flour
125g (1 cup) chopped walnuts

Preheat oven to 180°C. Grease a 20cm square cake tin and line base with baking paper.

Melt chocolate and butter together in saucepan over low heat. Cool slightly, then stir in sugar and add eggs one at a time. Add flour and walnuts and mix well.

Pour into prepared tin and bake for about 25 minutes. Remove from the oven and cool in the tin.

To serve, sift with icing sugar and cut into squares.

Dianne Beerling, Corinda

GRANDMA'S JAM DROPS

These are Grandma's, which she has cooked for about 60 years. She used to post them to me when I came to Brisbane to do my nursing training to make sure I was eating properly.

4 tablespoons butter, softened
1 egg, lightly beaten
80g (⅓ cup) caster sugar
½ teaspoon vanilla essence
210g (1½ cups) self-raising flour
pinch of salt
80g (¼ cup) raspberry jam

Preheat oven to 180°C. Lightly grease a baking tray.

Combine butter, egg, sugar and vanilla in a mixing bowl. Add flour and salt and mix well. Roll teaspoonfuls of the dough into balls and place onto baking tray. Flatten with a fork then make an indentation in the centre of each biscuit with your finger. Using a teaspoon, fill the indent with a little jam.

Bake for about 12 minutes or until light golden. Remove from the oven and cool the biscuits on a wire rack.

Maree Thomas, Karalee

OATIE BISCUITS

This variant of Anzac Biscuits is a hit with my family and does not last long enough to cool. As a child my daughter baked these for her friends whenever she could.

200g (2 cups) rolled oats
60g (½ cup) self-raising flour
60g (½ cup) plain flour
170g (¾ cup) caster sugar
40g (⅓ cup) sultanas or mixed fruit
½ teaspoon bicarbonate of soda
2 tablespoons boiling water
125g (½ cup) butter or margarine, melted
2 tablespoons golden syrup

Preheat oven to 160°C. Line a baking tray with baking paper.

Mix together the oats, flours, sugar and sultanas in a large bowl. Dissolve the bicarbonate of soda in the boiling water then add to the melted butter with the golden syrup. Pour butter mixture into the dry ingredients and mix well. Place teaspoonfuls on baking tray, allowing room to spread.

Bake for 15 minutes.

Karolyn Campbell, Cleveland

OATMEAL COOKIES

I've been making this recipe since July 1987, and the secret to the cookies' good flavour is the soaking of the raisins.

3 eggs, lightly beaten
125g (1 cup) raisins
1 teaspoon vanilla essence
250g (1 cup) butter
230g (1 cup) sugar
230g (1 cup, firmly packed) brown sugar
360g (2½ cups) plain flour
1 teaspoon salt
1 teaspoon cinnamon
2 teaspoons baking soda
200g (2 cups) rolled oats
120g (1 cup) chopped hazelnuts

Combine eggs, raisins and vanilla and allow to stand, covered with plastic wrap, for at least 1 hour. Line a baking tray with baking paper.

Cream together the butter and sugars. Sift together the flour, salt, cinnamon and baking soda and stir into the creamed mixture. Lastly, stir in the rolled oats and hazelnuts to make a stiff dough.

Drop teaspoonfuls of the mixture onto the baking tray and bake for 10–12 minutes or until lightly brown. Remove from the oven and cool the biscuits on a wire rack.

Note: Walnuts or pecans can be used instead of hazelnuts. The raisins can be soaked overnight if preferred.

Joan Bowman, Carseldine

Orange Coconut Biscuits

This recipe was a favourite when my three boys were young nearly 50 years ago. It makes a lot and is good for lunches.

125g (½ cup) butter
230g (1 cup) caster sugar
1 teaspoon finely grated orange zest
1 egg, lightly beaten
300g (2 cups) self-raising flour
¼ teaspoon salt
90g (1 cup) desiccated coconut
60ml (¼ cup) orange juice

Preheat oven to 180°C. Line a baking tray with baking paper.

Beat butter, sugar and orange zest until light and fluffy. Add the egg and beat again. Stir in the combined flour, salt and coconut alternately with the orange juice.

Place tablespoonfuls of the mixture on the tray and bake for 15 minutes or light golden. Remove from the oven and cool on a wire rack.

Pat Gray, Kallangur

PIKELETS

This recipe is adapted from the book which accompanied my electric mixer, purchased in 1964, and which I still use today. The original recipe did not cool the mixture before cooking or use the Copha but I find this makes the pikelets better.

150g (1 cup) self-raising flour
pinch salt
¼ teaspoon bicarbonate of soda
2 tablespoons sugar
125ml (½ cup) milk
1 teaspoon white vinegar
1 egg
1 dessertspoon butter, melted

Combine flour, salt, bicarbonate of soda and sugar in a mixing bowl. Combine milk and vinegar in a small bowl, then stir in the egg and melted butter and add to dry ingredients. Beat again to mix thoroughly. Place mixture in refrigerator overnight.

Heat frying pan until hot and lightly grease using Copha. Place spoonfuls of mixture in the pan and cook until bubbles appear on the surface. Flip pikelet and cook other side.

Serve while warm.

Janice Fletcher, Carindale

PEANUT CRISPS

*Mum has been making these for the family camping trips
for as long as I can remember and I'm now 50.*

125g (½ cup) margarine or butter
220g (1 cup) sugar
1 egg, lightly beaten
150g (1 cup) self-raising flour
1 teaspoon cocoa powder
1 teaspoon salt
240g (1½ cups) raw peanuts

Preheat oven to 180°C. Line a baking tray with baking paper.

Melt butter and stir in the sugar. Add egg and dry ingredients and mix well. Lastly, stir in the peanuts.

Place teaspoonfuls of mixture on the baking tray, leaving room to spread. Bake for 15 minutes.

Remove from the oven and cool biscuits on a wire rack.

Jeff Maccoll, Wynnum West

PEANUT BIKKIES

I would like to share with you a special recipe that my grandmother, Mrs Alice Bradshaw, made for our family as we were growing up and it still remains a firm favourite now.

This would have to be the very easiest bikkie recipe yet!

375g (1½ cups) peanut paste, either crunchy or smooth
1 egg, lightly beaten
230g (1 cup) sugar

Preheat your oven to 180°C. Line a baking tray with baking paper.

Combine all ingredients well in a mixing bowl. Roll teaspoonfuls of the mixture into balls and place on a baking tray. If desired the biscuits can be pressed with a fork for a fancy effect.

Bake for 15–20 minutes. Remove biscuits from the oven and cool on a wire rack.

Anne Rostedt, Holland Park West

SNICKERDOODLES

250g (1 cup) butter, softened
345g (1½ cups) caster sugar
2 eggs, lightly beaten
390g (2¾ cups) plain flour
2 teaspoons cream of tartar
1 teaspoon bicarbonate of soda
¼ teaspoon salt
2 teaspoons caster sugar, extra
2 teaspoons cinnamon

Preheat oven to 180°C. Lightly grease a baking tray.

Cream together the butter and sugar until light and fluffy, then beat in the eggs. Sift together the flour, cream of tartar, bicarbonate of soda and salt and stir into the butter mixture.

Roll teaspoonfuls of the dough into balls. Combine extra sugar and cinnamon and roll the balls in this mixture. Place the balls on the baking tray, leaving room to spread, and flatten slightly with a floured fork.

Bake for 10 minutes. Remove from the oven and rest on the tray for a few minutes before putting the biscuits on a wire rack to cool completely.

Ann Earle, Sinnamon Park

YoYos

I first tasted this biscuit back in 1964 when my future mother-in-law made them as a favourite of my husband. This recipe has been a regular in our family, and now a favourite with the grandchildren. So quick and easy to make.

175g (¾ cup) butter
50g (½ cup) icing sugar
few drops vanilla essence
175g (1¼ cups) plain flour
50g (½ cup) custard powder

Butter Filling
6 tablespoons icing sugar
1 tablespoon butter
1 tablespoon custard powder

Preheat oven to 180°C. Line a baking tray with baking paper.

Cream together the butter and icing sugar, stir in the vanilla, then sift in remaining dry ingredients. Mix well to form a soft dough.

Roll teaspoonfuls of mixture into balls. Place balls onto baking tray and flatten with a fork.

Bake for 20 minutes then remove and cool on the tray for 5 minutes before putting on a wire rack to cool completely.

For the butter filling, place all ingredients in a small bowl and beat to a creamy consistency.

When biscuits are cold, spread a little filling on the underside of a biscuit and top with another biscuit.

Pamela Martin, Monterey Keys

ANZAC AND ORANGE MARMALADE SLICE

This can be served hot or cold! I've also used it as a winter dessert.

100g (1 cup) rolled oats
210g (1½ cups) plain flour, sifted
230g (1 cup) firmly packed brown sugar
90g (1 cup) desiccated coconut
125g (½ cup) butter
2 tablespoons golden syrup
2 tablespoons water
½ teaspoon bicarbonate of soda
160g (½ cup) warmed orange marmalade

Preheat oven to 180°C. Grease and line a 19cm x 29cm slice pan with baking paper.

Combine rolled oats, flour, sugar and coconut in a large mixing bowl. Place butter, golden syrup and water in a small saucepan and heat until the butter melts. Add the bicarbonate of soda to the golden syrup mixture, then stir into the dry ingredients.

Press two-thirds of the mixture into the tin and then spread with the marmalade. Dot the remaining mixture on top of the marmalade and bake in the oven for 35 minutes or until firm on top.

Remove from the oven and allow to cool before cutting into squares.

Joan Bowman, Carseldine

APPLE SLICE

150g (1 cup) self-raising flour
90g (1 cup) desiccated coconut
115g (½ cup) caster sugar
125g (½ cup) butter, melted
1 teaspoon vanilla essence
250g (1 cup) sour cream
420g tin sliced pie apples, drained
1 tablespoon cinnamon sugar

Preheat oven to 160°C. Line a 16cm x 26cm tin with baking paper.

Combine flour, coconut and sugar in a mixing bowl. Add butter and vanilla and stir through. Press mixture into the tin and bake for 10–15 minutes. Remove from the oven and cool for 5 minutes.

Spread sour cream over the base and top with the apple slices. Sprinkle with the cinnamon sugar and return to the oven for another 10–15 minutes.

Serve warm or cold with vanilla ice cream.

Note: Apricot pie filling can be substituted for the apple. Sprinkle chopped almonds and a teaspoon of ground mace or nutmeg on top before baking.

Joan Bowman, Carseldine

APRICOT BISCUIT LOG

This recipe has been a talking point whenever I have made it. It is a family gem that I got from my husband's Aunty Sue. I understand that she is well known in her small town in South Australia for this little slice of heaven, and I loved it so much that I brought it with me when we moved to Brisbane. I make it often and it always get gobbled up!

200g (1¼ cups) dried apricots, chopped
100g (1 cup) marshmallows, chopped
250g sweet biscuits, crushed
400g tin condensed milk
4 tablespoons finely chopped mixed nuts
1 teaspoon vanilla essence
90g (1 cup) desiccated coconut for rolling

Place all ingredients except coconut into a bowl and mix well. Divide mixture into 4 and shape each portion into a log. Place logs in refrigerator to become firm. Remove from the refrigerator and roll in coconut.

To serve, cut into slices on the diagonal. Store the logs in the refrigerator or the freezer.

Stephanie Eaton, East Brisbane

CARAMEL FINGERS

125g (½ cup) butter
110g (1 cup) raw sugar
160 g (1 cup) chopped dates
2 eggs, lightly beaten
185ml (¾ cup) milk
300g (2 cups) self-raising flour
1 teaspoon vanilla essence
120g (1 cup) chopped pecans

ICING
1 dessertspoon instant coffee granules
3 tablespoons boiling water
1 dessertspoon butter
250g (2 cups) icing sugar

Preheat oven to 180°C. Line a 20cm x 25cm tin with baking paper.

Combine butter, sugar and dates in a saucepan and stir over a low heat until butter has melted. Pour mixture into a mixing bowl and stir in the eggs. Add remaining ingredients, except pecans, and mix well.

Spoon into tin and bake in the oven for 20 minutes or until golden brown. Remove from the oven and allow to cool in the tin.

For the icing, dissolve the instant coffee in the water. Cream the butter and icing sugar together in a mixing bowl and add enough coffee to make a spreading consistency, adding more liquid if necessary.

Spread icing over the slice and scatter with pecans. Slice into fingers to serve.

Dawn Letchford, Mudjimba

Caramel Marshmallow Slice

I make this for church stalls and it is very popular. Some people say it is the only reason they come out on voting day!

Base

150g (1 cup) self-raising flour
65g (¾ cup) desiccated coconut
125g (½ cup, lightly packed) brown sugar
125g (½ cup) butter, melted

Caramel

440g tin condensed milk
60g (¼ cup) butter
2 tablespoons golden syrup

Marshmallow

220g (1 cup) sugar
250ml (1 cup) water
1 tablespoon gelatine
squeeze lemon juice

1 tablespoon desiccated coconut

Preheat oven to 180°C. Grease a lamington tin.

Place all base ingredients in a mixing bowl and stir well to combine. Press the mixture into the lamington tin. Bake in oven until golden brown then remove and allow to cool completely.

For the caramel, place all ingredients in a saucepan and stir over moderate heat for about 15 minutes, until golden brown. Remove from heat and pour over the cooled base.

For the marshmallow, place all the ingredients in a saucepan and bring slowly to the boil, then reduce heat and simmer for 5 minutes. Remove from heat and allow mixture to cool until it's lukewarm.

Beat the mixture in an electric mixer, or with electric beaters, on a high speed until thick, adding a few drops of vanilla and food colouring if desired. Spread marshmallow topping over the caramel and sprinkle with coconut.

Adele Whisson, Bald Hills

CHINESE CHEWS

My mother's recipe and loved by all.

150 g (1 cup) plain flour
110 g (½ cup) sugar
pinch salt
1 teaspoon baking powder
160g (1 cup) dates, chopped
60g (½ cup) walnuts
2 eggs, lightly beaten
125 g (½ cup) butter, melted

Preheat oven to 180°C. Line a 20cm square tin with baking paper.

Combine dry ingredients in a mixing bowl, then add dates and walnuts. Stir in eggs and butter and mix well. Spoon the mixture into the tin and smooth the surface.

Bake for about 25 minutes or until firm on the top. Remove from the oven and cool in the tin before cutting into small squares.

Robin Baker, Burleigh Waters

CHOCOLATE COCONUT SLICE

This slice is really popular with all the family, I've been making it since the kids were young, and now make it for the grandchildren. It's very good for lunchboxes.

BASE

150g (1 cup) self-raising flour
125g (½ cup) butter, melted
55g (¼ cup) caster sugar
45g (½ cup) desiccated coconut

TOPPING

125g (1 cup) icing sugar
1 tablespoon cocoa powder
75g butter, melted
90g (1 cup) desiccated coconut
1–2 tablespoons milk

Preheat oven to 180°C. Line a 20cm square tin with baking paper.

Combine all base ingredients in a mixing bowl and press into the tin. Bake for 20 minutes.

For the topping, combine all the ingredients, adding more coconut if mixture is too runny. As soon as the base comes out of the oven, spread the topping over it. Allow to cool then refrigerate 1 hour.

Cut into slices.

Sue Gold, Woody Point

DATE AND NUT BARS

250g (1½ cups) chopped dates
75g (⅓ cup) brown sugar
60g (⅓ cup) wholemeal self-raising flour
60g (½ cup) chopped walnuts or pecans
1 teaspoon baking powder
1 teaspoon mixed spice
pinch salt
2 eggs, lightly beaten
60ml (¼ cup) vegetable oil
few drops vanilla essence
icing sugar for serving

Preheat oven to 180°C. Grease a 23cm square tin.

Place dry ingredients in a mixing bowl and stir to combine. Add eggs, vegetable oil and vanilla and mix well. Spoon mixture into the tin and press down with the back of a spoon.

Bake for 25 minutes or until golden brown and firm to touch. Remove from the oven and cut into bars while hot then set aside to cool completely.

Dust bars with icing sugar before serving.

Joan Bowman, Carseldine

DEANY'S GLUTEN-FREE SLUDGE SLICE

This recipe is special because my aunty kindly adapted it to be gluten free so I could enjoy it as much as the rest of the family. Everyone loves it just as much as a non-gluten-free recipe and it is so easy to make.

BASE
250g packet gluten-free sweet biscuits, crushed
150g (⅔ cup) butter, melted

CARAMEL
125g (½ cup) butter
185g (1 cup, lightly packed) brown sugar
400g tin condensed milk
2 tablespoons golden syrup

250g dark chocolate

Grease a 20cm square cake tin.

Combine the biscuit crumbs and butter in a mixing bowl, then press into the greased tin and refrigerate.

For the caramel, combine butter, sugar, condensed milk and golden syrup over a medium heat and continue stirring until just bubbling. Lower the heat and continue stirring for 10 minutes. Pour the mixture over the biscuit base.

Melt chocolate in a bowl set over boiling water, or in the microwave, stirring until smooth. Pour chocolate over caramel, allow to cool then refrigerate until set.

To serve, cut into slices.

Leah Fitzgerald-Quinn, Sinnamon Park

FRUIT SLICE

300g (2 cups) self-raising flour
230g (1 cup, tightly packed) brown sugar
125g (½ cup) butter
210g (¾ cup) raspberry jam, warmed
185g (1 cup) mixed fruit
½ teaspoon baking powder
½ teaspoon mixed spice
1 egg
150ml (¾ cup) of milk

Preheat oven to 180°C. Lightly grease an 18cm x 28cm lamington tin.

Combine flour and sugar in a mixing bowl and rub in the butter. Press half of this mixture into the slice tin and spread with the jam.

Stir the mixed fruit, baking powder, mixed spice, egg and milk into the remaining base mixture and pour over the jam. Bake for 25–30 minutes or until golden on top. Remove from the oven and allow to cool before cutting into fingers.

Joan Bowman, Carseldine

GINGER SLICE

This is from my Eighth Grade domestic science exercise book which was handwritten in 1958.

250g (1 cup) butter
125g (½ cup) caster sugar
125g (¾ cup) self-raising flour
125g (¾ cup) plain flour
2 teaspoons ground ginger
pinch salt

ICING
125g (1 cup) icing sugar
65g (¼ cup) butter, softened
1 tablespoon ground ginger
3 teaspoons golden syrup

Preheat oven to 180°C. Line a 20cm square tin with baking paper.

Cream the butter and sugar then add sifted flours, ginger and salt. Mix well. Spread mixture into tin and bake in the oven for 25–30 minutes.

For the icing, place all ingredients in a small saucepan and heat gently until the butter has melted. Stir until smooth. Spread icing mixture over base when it comes out of the oven and leave to cool.

To serve, cut into fingers.

Gai Aplin, Murrumba Downs

LEMON SLICE

This is so easy to make, and it was once a great favourite of the family. After many years of not making this I recently tried it again and it has become a hit with family and friends once more. It's a fantastic treat when using the gluten-free biscuits for my daughter and two granddaughters who need a gluten-free diet.

250g packet plain gluten-free biscuits
125g Copha
400g tin condensed milk
90g (1 cup) desiccated coconut
125ml (½ cup) lemon juice

ICING
125g (1 cup) icing sugar
1 teaspoon lemon juice
1 tablespoon Copha
½ tablespoon boiling water

Line a 18cm x 28cm lamington tin with baking paper.

Place half the biscuits in the tray. Melt the Copha, allow to cool. Combine melted Copha, condensed milk, coconut and lemon juice in a mixing bowl and stir until smooth. Spread mixture over the biscuits then top with remaining biscuits.

For the icing, combine all ingredients and beat until smooth. Spread over the slice and refrigerate to set.

Pamela Martin, Monterey Keys

MELT-AND-MIX CHOCOLATE SLICE

125g (½ cup) butter, melted
115g (½ cup) brown sugar
190g (1⅓ cup) plain flour

TOPPING
200g milk chocolate
2 eggs, lightly beaten
140g (¾ cup, lightly packed) brown sugar
2 tablespoons plain flour
45g (½ cup) desiccated coconut
100 g (¾ cup) slivered almonds

Preheat oven to 180°C. Grease and line a 25cm square tin with baking paper.

Combine butter, sugar and flour in bowl and mix well. Press mixture into slice tin and bake for 14–16 minutes until golden.

For the topping, melt the chocolate in a glass bowl over simmering water or in the microwave. Let it cool slightly, then add eggs and stir well before adding sugar, flour, coconut and almonds. Spread topping over the base and bake for 18 minutes or until firm to touch. Remove from the oven and allow to cool before cutting into squares.

Joan Macrow, Eight Mile Plains

MUESLI SLICE

This slice is suitable for people on a gluten-free diet.

400g tin condensed milk
250g (2½ cups) rolled oats
125g (¾ cup) raw peanuts
125g (1 cup) mixed seeds such as pumpkin, sesame, sunflowers etc.
100g (¾ cup) dried fruit
75g (¾ cup) desiccated coconut

Preheat oven to 150°C. Line a 20cm square tin with baking paper.

Place the condensed milk in a glass bowl and warm in the microwave.
Add remaining ingredients and mix well.

Press mixture into the tin and bake for 1 hour or until golden brown.

Carolyn Goldsmith, Sunnybank Hills

MUNCHIES

180g (2 cups) desiccated coconut
220g (1 cup) sugar
150g (1 cup) plain flour
100g (1 cup) rolled oats
125g (½ cup) butter
2 tablespoons boiling water
1 tablespoon golden syrup
1 teaspoon bicarbonate of soda

Preheat oven to 160°C. Line a 25cm x 30cm lamington tin with baking paper.

Combine coconut, sugar, flour and oats in a large mixing bowl. Place butter, water and golden syrup in a small saucepan and stir over medium heat until the butter has melted. Stir in bicarbonate of soda. Pour butter mixture over the dry ingredients and stir to combine.

Spoon mixture into the tin, pressing down firmly. Bake for 20 minutes.

Remove from the oven and rest for 5 minutes before cutting into squares but leave in the tin until completely cold.

Valerie Landells, Kings Beach

RASPBERRY SQUARES

When visiting Newfoundland some years ago I was welcomed at a B&B with a cup of tea and this slice.

200g (2 cups) quick oats
185g (1 cup) brown sugar
150g (1 cup) plain flour
1 teaspoon baking powder
185g (¾ cup) butter, melted
240g (¾ cup) raspberry jam

Preheat oven to 180°C. Lightly grease a 20cm x 30cm lamington tin and line with baking paper.

Combine oats, sugar, flour and baking powder in a mixing bowl. Add the melted butter and mix well. Press half the mixture into the tin and spread with a layer of jam.

Crumble over the remaining mixture and bake for 30 minutes.

Remove from the oven and cool in the tin before cutting into squares.

Pat Gray, Kallangur

ALLERGY-FREE CHOCOLATE CAKE

This cake recipe is egg-, dairy- and nut-free and is great for children and adults alike with special dietary requirements.

360g (2½ cups) plain flour
125g (1 cup) nut-free cocoa powder
2 teaspoons bicarbonate of soda
½ teaspoon salt
395g (1¾ cups, firmly packed) light brown sugar
500ml (2 cups) soy milk
85ml (⅓ cup) nut-free vegetable oil (not olive oil)
1 tablespoon white vinegar
1 teaspoon vanilla extract
425g tin stoneless black cherries, drained
2 tablespoons cherry jam, approximately

Preheat oven to 180°C. Lightly grease two 20cm round tins and line with baking paper.

Sift together the flour, cocoa powder, bicarbonate of soda and salt. Stir in the sugar. In another bowl, combine the soy milk, oil, vinegar and vanilla then stir into the dry ingredients and mix well. Divide mixture between the two tins and place cherries over the top.

Bake for 35–40 minutes or until the centre springs back when lightly touched. Remove from the oven and leave to cool in the tins for 10 minutes before turning out on a wire cooling rack to cool completely.

Place one sponge cake on a serving plate and spread with cherry jam. Place the other sponge on top and spread chocolate ganache or chocolate buttercream evenly over the top and sides of the cake.

Chocolate Ganache
125ml (½ cup) soy cream
115g (½ cup) caster sugar
200 g nut- and dairy-free dark chocolate, chopped
1 teaspoon cherry or chocolate liqueur

Combine cream and sugar in a small saucepan and heat to boiling point. Remove from heat and stir in chocolate until it melts and the mixture becomes smooth. Stir in liqueur. Allow to cool before using.

Chocolate Buttercream
175g (¾ cup) dairy-free spread
1 teaspoon vanilla extract
400g (3¼ cups) icing sugar
125g (1 cup) nut-free cocoa powder

Whip the spread and vanilla to soften. Sift together the sugar and cocoa powder and gradually stir into the butter mixture until smooth.

Belinda Dennis, Alderley

APPLE, SULTANA AND BANANA CAKE

This cake is so easy – it is made in one bowl and does not require an electric mixer. This recipe came from my late mother's hand-written recipe collection, some 50 years ago.

250g (2 cups) self-raising flour
1 teaspoon mixed spice
125g (½ cup) butter or margarine
125g (½ cup) caster sugar
1 egg, lightly beaten
225g Granny Smith apples, peeled, cored and chopped
100g (¾ cup) sultanas
2 large bananas, chopped
1 tablespoon brown sugar
½ teaspoon cinnamon

Preheat oven to 190°C. Grease a 23cm round cake tin and line with baking paper.

Sift flour and mixed spice into large bowl and rub in butter until mixture resembles breadcrumbs. Add caster sugar and egg and stir well. Stir in apples, sultanas and bananas. Mixture should be dropping consistency but if too dry then add a little milk.

Spoon mixture into the tin and bake for 50–60 minutes. Remove from the oven and sprinkle over the combined brown sugar and cinnamon while the cake is hot. Cool on a wire rack.

Carol Robinson, Karana Downs

BRISBANE FLOOD MUD CAKE

375g (2½ cups) white chocolate buttons
80g (⅓ cup) butter
250ml (1 cup) milk
8 level tablespoons sugar
3 teaspoons instant coffee granules
3 teaspoons boiling water
3 eggs
2 teaspoons vanilla extract
150g (1 cup) self-raising flour
85g (⅔ cup) plain flour

FROSTING
185g (1¼ cups) white chocolate buttons
2 tablespoons sour cream
3 tablespoons icing sugar
instant coffee granules or cocoa powder

Preheat oven to 180°C. Grease a 20cm cake tin and line with baking paper.

Place white chocolate, butter, milk and sugar in a saucepan and stir over low heat until chocolate has melted. Remove from heat and allow to cool for 20 minutes. Dissolve coffee granules in boiling water and stir into chocolate mixture. Whisk together the eggs and vanilla and add to the chocolate mixture.

Sift together the flours into a large mixing bowl and slowly add the chocolate mixture, stirring to a smooth batter. Pour into prepared tin.

Reduce oven to 175°C and bake cake for 1¼ hours. To test if the cake is cooked, insert a skewer into the centre of the cake – it should come out clean. The centre of the cake should be firm.

For the frosting, melt the white chocolate in the microwave, or in a bowl set over a saucepan of simmering water, before adding remaining ingredients and beating until smooth. The coffee granules or cocoa powder are to make the frosting the colour of brown mud, so start with ½ teaspoon and add more if necessary.

Patricia Sparrow, Russell Island

BANANA HEALTH LOAF

My big sister gave this recipe to me many years ago, when I was a young mum of 3. It just brings back some lovely memories. I hope you like it as much as we all did.

1 cup bran cereal
250ml (1 cup) milk
150g (1 cup) wholemeal self-raising flour
1 teaspoon bicarbonate of soda
110g (½ cup) raw sugar
90g (½ cup) apricots, chopped
60g (½ cup) sultanas
90g (1 cup) desiccated coconut
45g (½ cup) wheatgerm
3 bananas, mashed
2 eggs, lightly beaten

Preheat oven to 170°C. Grease a loaf tin and line with baking paper. In a large bowl, cover bran cereal with milk and soak for 10–15 minutes.

Combine flour, bicarbonate of soda, sugar, apricots, sultanas, coconut and wheatgerm in a bowl and stir well. Combine bananas and eggs in a small bowl. Add banana mixture to soaked bran mixture, then add remaining dry ingredients and mix well. Spoon mixture into the loaf tin and smooth the surface.

Bake for 1 hour or until a skewer inserted into the centre of the cake comes out clean.

Kerrie Roofayel, Albany Creek

BUTTER CAKE

Growing up, this cake was a staple in our home and there was always one, or a portion of one, in Mum's cake tin. My mother would sometimes convert it into a marble cake, a chocolate cake or put fruit on top. Absolutely delicious. Don't be tempted to use margarine instead of butter as you won't get that rich, old-fashioned flavour.

4 eggs
250g (1 cup) butter
250g (1¾ cups) self-raising flour
250g (1 cup) caster sugar
few drops vanilla essence

Preheat oven to 180°C. Grease a 20cm cake tin and line with baking paper.

Place all ingredients into food processor and mix until smooth. Pour mixture into the tin and bake for 40 minutes.

Remove from the oven and rest for 3 minutes before turning out on a wire rack to cool completely.

Note: This cake can be topped with tinned fruit such as apricots or cherries before baking. Toss fruit in a little flour to stop it sinking into the batter before evenly spreading on top of cake mixture.

Heather Deane, Wynnum

CARROT CAKE

There are lots of mediocre carrot cakes out there. This one is truly fantastic – the icing should be illegal it is so good.

300g (2 cups) plain flour
230g (1 cup) caster sugar
2 teaspoons baking powder
1 teaspoon salt
4 eggs, lightly beaten
300g (2 cups, firmly packed) grated carrot
425g tin crushed pineapple, well drained
125g (1 cup) chopped walnuts
250ml (1 cup) vegetable oil

ICING
180g (¾ cup) butter
250g (1 cup) cream cheese
360g (3 cups) icing sugar
1 teaspoon vanilla
40g (⅓ cup) chopped walnuts

Preheat oven to 160°C. Grease a 24cm cake tin and line with baking paper.

Combine dry ingredients in a large mixing bowl. Add eggs, carrot, pineapple, walnuts and half the oil. Mix well. If batter is wet enough then do not add more oil. If it is a bit dry, gradually add the remaining oil and mix it in very well.

Pour batter into the tin and cook for 1 hour or until a skewer inserted into the centre of the cake comes out clean.

For the icing, beat the butter, cream cheese, icing sugar and vanilla together until smooth. Spread over the cooled cake and sprinkle with the walnuts.

Belinda McBride, The Gap

CHOCOLATE CAKE WITH A TOUCH OF BEETROOT

SES Western Group was heavily involved in the floods, even having to evacuate ourselves from our flooding depot at Toowong to the auditorium at Mt Coot-Tha.

After hours volunteering alongside each other to help the flood victims of Brisbane, we shared a relaxing afternoon to farewell one of our treasured members who was moving interstate.

This recipe became the centrepiece of our bring-a-plate picnic at Mt Coot-Tha Botanical Gardens as we reflected on a big two weeks of floods and storms, and enjoyed being together – this time relaxing – in a Brisbane landmark that had become so central to our lives in the preceding weeks.

250g good dark chocolate, broken into pieces
250g (1 cup) unsalted butter, cubed
3 eggs
250g (1 cup) caster sugar
150g (1 cup) self-raising flour
250g beetroot, peeled and grated

Preheat oven 180°C. Grease a 20cm x 30cm cake tin and line with baking paper.

Place chocolate and butter in a bowl and either melt in the microwave or over a saucepan of simmering water, stirring frequently. Whisk together eggs and sugar, then beat in cooled chocolate mixture until smooth. Gently fold in flour and beetroot.

Pour mixture into prepared tin and bake for 30 minutes or until a skewer inserted into the centre of the cake comes out clean.

SES Western Group, Toowong

CHOCOLATE AND PISTACHIO CAKE

This recipe is special because it never fails to please.

16 sweet biscuits, roughly broken
210g (1½ cups) raw pistachio kernels
345g (1½ cups) caster sugar
2 teaspoons baking powder
180g white chocolate, chopped
8 egg whites
2 tablespoons icing sugar
thick cream, to serve

Preheat oven to 180°C. Grease a 24cm springform tin and line with baking paper.

Process biscuits and pistachios in a food processor until chopped but not as fine as breadcrumbs. Transfer to a large bowl. Add sugar, baking powder and chocolate and stir until well combined.

Using an electric mixer, beat egg whites on high speed until stiff peaks form. Add a third of the egg whites to the dry ingredients and fold to combine. Add remaining egg whites and gently fold through. Spoon the mixture into the springform tin.

Bake for 40–45 minutes or until the cake is light golden and firm to touch in the centre. Turn off the oven and allow to cool completely with door ajar.

Remove cake from the tin and place on serving plate. Dust with icing sugar and serve with thick cream.

Leanne Byrne, Aspley

DATE TEA CAKE

My mother (born 1910) used to make this often for morning and afternoon tea. I came across it recently and made it for my friends, and it was a great hit.

300g (2 cups) self-raising flour
pinch salt
2 tablespoons butter
2 heaped tablespoons brown sugar
160g (1 cup) chopped dates
185g (1 cup) mixed fruit
1 egg
60ml (¾ cup) milk
approximately 1 tablespoon sugar, extra

Preheat oven to 180°C. Grease a 20cm cake tin and line with baking paper.

Sift together flour and salt and rub in the butter until mixture resembles breadcrumbs. Add sugar, dates and mixed fruit and stir to combine. Lightly beat egg into milk and stir mixture into dry ingredients. Pour batter into tin and sprinkle top with extra sugar.

Bake for about 35–40 minutes or until a skewer inserted into the centre comes out clean. Remove from the oven and cool on a wire rack.

To serve, cut into slices and spread with butter.

Jill Hislop, Sinnamon Park

DATE, GINGER AND CARROT CAKE

By trial and error I have arrived at what I think is a quite delicious gluten- and dairy-free cake. I sometimes use almond or macadamia meal instead of the hazelnut. I have also used pumpkin instead of carrot.

360g (2 cups) dates, chopped
380g (2 cups) crystallised ginger, chopped
300g (2 cups) grated carrot
250ml (1 cup) macadamia oil
60ml (¼ cup) rum or brandy
2 teaspoons baking powder
300g (2 cups) hazelnut meal
5 eggs, lightly beaten
145g (⅔ cup) caster sugar

Preheat the oven to 170°C. Grease a 23cm springform tin and line with baking paper.

Combine dates, ginger, carrot, oil and rum in a large saucepan and bring to the boil. Reduce heat and simmer until dates have softened. Remove the saucepan from the heat, stir in baking powder and allow to cool. Then add the hazelnut meal to the cake mixture and stir through. Beat the eggs and sugar until light and fluffy and gently fold through the batter.

Pour mixture into the cake tin and bake for 1 hour, or until a skewer inserted into the centre of the cake comes out clean.

Joan Skinner, Red Hill

DIGELLA'S CUPCAKES

These cupcakes have been adapted from a recipe by my idol Nigella Lawson and are my favourite recipe of all time. These simple little cakes scored me the name Digella from work colleagues. Since turning home baker in 2006 these cupcakes have been provided in abundance at many events and, due to my passion, Baked Relief was born. Put simply, a cupcake is life changing.

250g (1 cup) unsalted butter
250g (1 cup) caster sugar
250g (1¾ cups) self-raising flour
4 large eggs
1 teaspoon vanilla extract
5 tablespoons of milk

BUTTERCREAM ICING
125g (½ cup) unsalted butter, at room temperature
200 g (1¾ cups) icing mixture, sifted
1 teaspoon vanilla essence
1 tablespoons of milk

Preheat oven to 200°C. Line 24 cupcake tins with papers.

Put all the ingredients except the milk into a food processor and blitz until smooth. Keep the processor running while you add the milk down the funnel.

Divide mixture among the papers and bake in oven for 15–20 minutes, taking care not to overcook – a little underdone makes for a nice moist cake. Remove cakes from the oven and allow to cool on a wire rack.

For the buttercream icing, cream the butter until very pale – almost white – in colour, scraping down the sides of the bowl a couple of times. Add about half the sifted icing mixture and beat until combined. Add vanilla, milk and remaining sifted icing mixture.

Ice cooled cakes and decorate with a sweet little icing rose, some sprinkles or even a berry.

Note: Food colouring may be added to the buttercream icing if desired.

Danielle Crismani, Mitchelton

DOREEN'S COCONUT CAKE

A dense but delicious cake which will last several days if not eaten immediately.

210g (1½ cups) self-raising flour
115g (½ cup) sugar
60g (⅔ cup) desiccated coconut
125g (½ cup) butter
2 eggs
60ml (⅓ cup) milk
1–2 teaspoons vanilla essence

CHOCOLATE ICING
185g (1½ cups) icing sugar
2 tablespoons cocoa powder
1 dessertspoon butter
1 tablespoon hot milk

Preheat oven to 180°C. Grease a 20cm cake tin and line with baking paper.

Combine the flour, sugar and coconut in a large bowl. Melt the butter and let it cool slightly before beating in the eggs and milk. Add wet ingredients to dry and mix well.

Pour batter into prepared tin and bake for 30–35 minutes, or until a skewer inserted into the centre of the cake comes out clean.

For the chocolate icing, sift together the icing sugar and cocoa powder. Beat in butter and enough hot milk to obtain a spreading consistency.

Spread the chocolate icing over the cooled cake. Lemon icing is also good with this cake.

Claire Stephens, Sunrise Beach

Easy Date Loaf

This cake does not contain any sugar or eggs and is suitable for people on special diets.

2 teaspoons instant coffee granules
250ml (1 cup) boiling water
375g (2⅓ cups) dates, chopped
150g (1 cup) self-raising flour
40g (¼ cup) flaked almonds or chopped walnuts

Preheat oven to 160°C. Grease a loaf tin and line with baking paper.

Dissolve coffee granules in the boiling water, pour over dates and leave to soak overnight.

Stir sifted flour into the dates and add a little water if the mixture is too dry. Spoon the mixture into the loaf tin and sprinkle the nuts over the top.

Bake for 45 minutes or until firm on top and a skewer inserted into the centre of the cake comes out clean. Remove from the oven and leave in the tin for 10 minutes before turning out onto a wire rack to cool completely.

Jan Rhoades, Upper Mt Gravatt

EGG-, NUT- AND DAIRY-FREE CUPCAKES

My two beautiful children are both allergic to nuts and this recipe is ideal for their special diets. It's cheap, cheerful and could encourage people to consider those who are less lucky than themselves. It has no 'special' ingredients and is therefore perfect, as most people will have everything they need already in their pantry.

210g (1½ cups) self-raising flour
230g (1 cup) caster sugar
1 teaspoon vanilla essence
125ml (½ cup) canola oil
3 tablespoons cocoa powder
250ml (1 cup) water
1 tablespoon white vinegar

Preheat oven to 190°C. Line a 12-cup cupcake tin with papers.

Combine all ingredients in the bowl of an electric mixer and beat for 3 minutes, until it is smooth and a dropping consistency. Spoon mixture into cupcake tin and bake for 12–15 minutes.

Remove from the oven and place the cupcakes on a wire rack to cool completely.

The cakes can be iced with a butter-free icing or decorated with allergy-free sweets.

Note: This recipe can be made as one whole cake but make sure you cook in a slower oven and for a longer time.

Gai Woolrych, Grange

FLOURLESS ORANGE CHOCOLATE CAKE

CAKE

200g dark chocolate (70% cocoa solids), roughly chopped
140g butter
200g sugar
1 tablespoon orange-flavoured liqueur
4 eggs, separated
35g (⅓ cup) almond meal
1½ tablespoons orange zest
2 tablespoons freshly squeezed orange juice with pulp

ORANGE SYRUP

110g (½ cup) sugar
60ml (¼ cup) water
1 tablespoon orange zest
2 tablespoons freshly squeezed orange juice

Preheat oven to 170°C. Grease 23cm round cake tin and line with baking paper. If using a springform tin, line with foil to avoid leakage.

Melt the chocolate and butter together in a small pan over a low heat. Stir in half the sugar and the liqueur. Set aside to cool to room temperature then beat in the egg yolks.

Beat egg whites until medium peaks form. Add remaining sugar and beat for 3 minutes until the meringue mixture is glossy.

Add almond meal, orange zest and orange juice to the chocolate mixture and mix well. Gently fold the meringue into the chocolate mixture, ensuring it is well mixed with no white meringue showing.

Pour mixture into the cake tin and bake for 40–50 minutes or until set.

Remove the cake from the oven but cool in the tin; the cake can be refrigerated for a few hours.

For the orange syrup, place the sugar and water in a small saucepan and cook on a low heat until sugar has dissolved. Add orange zest and juice, stir to combine and set aside to cool.

To serve, remove the cake from the tin, cut into slices and drizzle with the cooled orange syrup.

Sharon Swaine, Doncaster

GINGER CAKE

I made many of these cakes to take to people who were affected by the floods as it is a very easy recipe to duplicate. Of all the cakes that I have brought in to the studios of 612 ABC Brisbane for the segments with Madonna King, I think this has been the favourite.

390g (2¾ cups) self-raising flour
1 teaspoon bicarbonate of soda
3 teaspoons ground ginger
250ml (1 cup) warm water
115g (½ cup) dark brown sugar, firmly packed
125g (½ cup) butter, melted
260g (¾ cup) golden syrup
1 egg

Preheat oven to 160°C. Line a shallow 30cm x 20cm or deep 23cm square cake tin with baking paper.

Place all remaining ingredients into a food processor and process until smooth – do not overprocess. Pour batter into prepared tin and smooth the top.

Bake for 45 minutes or until the cake springs back when lightly touched and a wooden skewer inserted into the centre of the cake comes out clean. Remove from oven and allow to cool on a wire rack.

VARIATIONS:

Add ⅓ cup finely chopped glace ginger.

Add 1 cup chopped dates to the cake mixture.

Try using different spice mixtures e.g. 1 teaspoon cinnamon, 1 teaspoon ginger, ½ teaspoon allspice.

Use different shaped tins e.g. 8cm round fluted tins, 13cm x 8cm rectangular tins, small petit-four cases, baby muffin trays or loaf tins.

Dust with icing sugar or top with lime or lemon icing.

Alison Alexander, Karana Downs

GOOD FOR YOU MUFFINS

I received this recipe in Adelaide from my dear friend Bevaley on 2nd August 2003.

2½ teaspoons bicarbonate of soda
250ml (1 cup) boiling water
125g (½ cup) butter
230g (1 cup) sugar
2 eggs
360g (2½ cups) plain flour
½ teaspoon salt
500ml (2 cups) milk
75g (1 cup) unprocessed bran
2 cups bran cereal
160g (1 cup) chopped dates
60g (½ cup) chopped walnuts

Preheat oven to 190°C. Lightly grease three 12-cup muffin trays.

Combine bicarbonate of soda with hot water and set aside to cool. Cream butter and sugar until light and fluffy then add eggs one at a time. Stir in flour and salt alternately with the milk. Add the bicarbonate of soda liquid and the remaining ingredients. Mix well.

Spoon the mixture into the muffin trays, filling each cup to about three-quarters. Bake for 15–20 minutes then remove and turn out onto a wire rack to cool completely.

Note: 1 teaspoon cinnamon or nutmeg or ½ teaspoon allspice can be sifted with the flour. This mixture can be made ahead and stored in the refrigerator.

Joan Bowman, Carseldine

GREENWOOD CHOCOLATE CAKE

This was a stand-by of my mother's, and made its appearance on school cake stalls and afternoon teas for many years. It's fairly simple to make, the only unusual thing about it is the addition of a quarter cup of boiling water. I hope it might put a bit of sustenance and sweetness into peoples' lives.

125 g (½ cup) butter
230g (1 cup) caster sugar
2 eggs
210g (1½ cups) self-raising flour
pinch of bicarbonate of soda
pinch salt
1 tablespoon cocoa or 2 tablespoons drinking chocolate
125ml (½ cup) milk
½ teaspoon vanilla
60ml (¼ cup) boiling water

Preheat oven to 180°C. Grease and flour two 20cm cake tins and line with baking paper.

Cream butter and sugar until light and fluffy. Add eggs one at a time and beat in thoroughly. Sift flour, bicarbonate of soda and salt. Dissolve cocoa in milk with the vanilla essence. Add dry ingredients alternately with the milk mixture to the butter mixture. Lastly, mix in boiling water.

Spoon mixture into tins and bake for 30 minutes or until a skewer inserted into the centre of the cakes comes out clean. Remove from the oven and leave for a few minutes before turning the cakes out onto a wire rack to cool completely.

Cakes may be left plain or iced with the Best Ever Icing page 186. They may also be sandwiched together with cream or icing.

Helen Derrick, Sherwood

HESTER'S BOILED FRUIT CAKE

The following recipe is one handed down to my mother-in-law, who passed it onto me just after my marriage almost 48 years ago. This simple fruit cake recipe has been a family favourite and one which, if I want to build credits with my husband, I will bake and know it does the trick!

When my husband, Gordon, was serving in Vietnam in 1968, I used to bake this cake and send it over to him. My eldest son, Stuart, also regularly received this cake when he was serving in Iraq in 2008. Stuart is currently based south-west of Gaza and enjoys receiving a parcel with the cake, which he says arrives still moist. In fact I have just baked another and it is ready to parcel up and post.

500g (4 cups) mixed fruit
250g (1 cup) butter, chopped
230g (1 cup) caster sugar
250ml (1 cup) water
1 teaspoon vanilla essence
2 eggs, lightly beaten
150g (1 cup) plain flour
150g (1 cup) self-raising flour
1 teaspoon bicarbonate of soda

Preheat oven to 180°C. Grease a 22cm cake tin and line with baking paper.

Combine mixed fruit, butter, sugar, water and vanilla in a saucepan and gently bring to the boil. Remove from the heat and allow to cool for 10 minutes.

Stir in the eggs, mixing well. Sift together the flours and bicarbonate of soda and stir into the fruit mixture.

Pour batter into the tin and bake in the oven for 1¼ hours. Remove from the oven and allow to cool in the tin before turning out.

Shirley Graham, Redland Bay

ISRAELI HONEY CAKE

Honey cake is eaten at Jewish New Year to hope for a sweet and peaceful year. There are many recipes for honey cake but this is the best in my opinion.

4 eggs
185g (1 cup) brown sugar
250ml (1 cup) vegetable oil
250ml (1 cup) strong black coffee
250ml (1 cup) honey
360g (2½ cups) self-raising flour
pinch salt
1 teaspoon allspice
1 teaspoon cinnamon

Preheat oven to 170°C. Lightly grease a large fluted or 25cm round cake tin.

Beat the eggs, sugar and oil until the sugar dissolves. Add coffee and honey and mix well. Sift together the flour, salt and spices and fold into the egg mixture.

Pour mixture into tin and bake in the oven for 1–1¼ hours. Remove from the oven and cool on a wire rack.

Note: This cake does not require icing and freezes well.

Suzanne Quintner, Bardon

LOVE CAKE

The cooking time specified is a bit open-ended. This cake comes out of the oven soft and firms up as it cools. Obviously if the mixture is still mostly liquid then it is not cooked yet, but a shallow wet patch under the top is OK. It might take a couple of goes to get it right with your oven – but 'failures' are still quite tasty.

3 eggs
460g (2 cups) caster sugar
150g (⅔ cup) butter, softened
250g (1⅔ cups) cashews, coarsely chopped
250g (2 cups) semolina
60ml (¼ cup) honey
1 teaspoon ground cinnamon
¼ teaspoon ground nutmeg
1 teaspoon ground cardamom

Preheat oven to 150°C. Grease a 20cm x 30cm cake tin and line with baking paper.

Beat eggs and sugar on high speed for 10 minutes until thick and light. Add softened butter and beat well. Stir in cashews, semolina, honey and spices. Spoon mixture into tin and bake for 1 hour or until golden on top. If cake browns too quickly on top, cover loosely with foil while baking.

Leave cake in tin to cool before cutting into small squares to serve.

Note: Almonds can be used instead of cashews. Increase spice quantities if preferred.

Michael Webster, Albion

MANGO FRUIT CAKE

I've had this recipe for possibly 20 years or so and I tore it out of a magazine but as it was so long ago I couldn't name which one. My family and friends love it as it is so moist and not too expensive as far as ingredients are concerned, and is basically a no-fail recipe.

425g tin mango slices in natural juice, chopped, juice reserved
500g (4 cups) dried mixed fruit
125ml (½ cup) water
210g (1½ cups) self-raising flour
1½ teaspoons bicarbonate of soda
2 eggs, lightly beaten

Preheat oven to 160°C. Grease or line base and sides of a 25cm x 15cm loaf tin.

Place the mango juice, mixed fruit and water in a saucepan and bring to the boil. Reduce heat and simmer uncovered for 1 minute. Remove from the heat and allow to cool to room temperature.

Sift together the flour and bicarbonate of soda and stir into the fruit mixture with the eggs and mango pieces, combining well. Pour mixture into the loaf tin and smooth the top.

Bake for 1 hour or until a skewer inserted into the centre of the cake comes out clean. Allow to cool completely in the pan.

If the top of the cake starts to darken too much, lightly cover with a piece of foil.

Kay Vidovich, Woolloongabba

MUFFIN MAGIC

We have used this recipe for 12 years at Centenary State High School with the Year 8 home economics students – it is never-fail and really easy and quick to make.

BASIC MUFFIN RECIPE
150g (1 cup) self-raising flour
150g (1 cup) wholemeal self-raising flour
1 egg
185ml (¾ cup) milk
125ml (½ cup) vegetable oil

Preheat oven to 180°C. Line a 12-cup muffin tray.

Combine the flours in a large mixing bowl. Mix egg, milk and oil in a separate bowl, then pour wet ingredients into dry ingredients and mix gently with a fork until mixture is only just combined – it will still have some lumps. Be careful not to overmix.

Fill each cup in the muffin tray three-quarters full and bake for 20–25 minutes.

VARIATIONS:
BLUEBERRY OR RASPBERRY MUFFINS
Stir 165g (¾ cup) brown sugar and 1 cup frozen blueberries or raspberries into flour before adding wet ingredients.

BANANA MUFFINS
Stir 165g (¾ cup) brown sugar into flour. Add 2 mashed bananas to wet ingredients before combining with dry ingredients.

Apple, Walnut and Cinnamon Muffins

Stir 165g (¾ cup) brown sugar, 2 teaspoons cinnamon, 60g (½ cup) chopped walnuts and 1 peeled and chopped apple into flour before adding wet ingredients.

Date Muffins

Stir 165g (¾ cup) brown sugar, 2 or 3 teaspoons mixed spice and 80g (½ cup) chopped dried dates into flour before adding wet ingredients.

Cheese and Corn Muffins

Stir 150g (1 cup) grated tasty cheese, 1 finely sliced shallot and a pinch of pepper into flour, then add 250g (1 cup) creamed corn and 1 tablespoon seeded mustard to wet ingredients before combining with dry ingredients.

Ham and cheese muffins

Stir ½ teaspoon chicken stock powder, ½ teaspoon hot paprika, 4 slices chopped ham or shortcut bacon and 150g (1 cup) grated tasty cheese into flour before adding wet ingredients.

Tomato, zucchini and basil muffins

Stir 135g (1 cup) grated zucchini, 20g (⅓ cup) chopped fresh basil and a pinch of pepper into dry ingredients, then add 2 tablespoons tomato paste to wet ingredients bowl and combine with dry ingredients.

Centenary State High School, Jindalee – Home Economics Department

MUM'S PUMPKIN FRUIT CAKE

My wonderful mother has been cooking this cake longer than the 41 years I've been alive and it is the most delicious fruit cake I have ever tasted. No one else I know makes a pumpkin fruit cake like this – don't know why!

Unlike so many other fruit cakes, it is not a 'heavy' fruit cake and eating a slice of it is like a piece of sunshine. So gorgeous, and you can't just stop at one piece.

Mum and Dad have raised five children, given selflessly all their lives to us, their many grandchildren and great-grand child. I grew up smelling this beautiful cake in our house and it takes me back to the very happy childhood I had in Silkwood, far north Queensland.

Mum and Dad are veterans of many a cyclone now and they survived Yasi just fine and will, I expect, experience a few more yet. They are the people I admire the most and I love them dearly.

500g (4 cups) mixed fruit
125g (½ cup) butter, chopped
230g (1 cup) caster sugar
250ml (1 cup) cold water
2 tablespoons golden syrup
1 teaspoon bicarbonate of soda
2 eggs, lightly beaten
250g (1 cup) cold, cooked, mashed pumpkin
150g (1 cup) self-raising flour
150g (1 cup) plain flour

Preheat oven to 180°C. Line a 23cm round cake tin with 2 layers of baking paper on the base and 1 layer on the sides of the tin.

Combine mixed fruit, butter, sugar, water, golden syrup and bicarbonate of soda in a saucepan and simmer, covered, for 20 minutes. Remove from the heat and allow to cool for 30 minutes.

Add beaten eggs and mashed pumpkin to fruit mixture and stir through. Sift together the flours and stir into the fruit mixture. Spoon batter into the tin and bake for about 1½ hours, or until cooked when tested with a skewer.

Remove from the oven and leave to cool in the tin before turning out.

Joanne Gilshenan, Regents Park

NANA H'S CHOCOLATE CAKE

This unusually different chocolate cake was originally from my great-grandmother's cookbook and has been cooked by the family for many years. My mother remembers eating this as a child so the recipe is quite possibly over 70 years old.

125g (½ cup) butter
230g (1 cup) sugar
1 egg, lightly beaten
300g (2 cups) plain flour
2 tablespoons cocoa powder
1 teaspoon baking powder
1 teaspoon cinnamon
250ml (1 cup) milk
1 teaspoon bicarbonate of soda
2 tablespoons golden syrup

Preheat oven to 180°C. Grease a 23cm cake tin and line with baking paper.

Cream butter and sugar until light and fluffy, add egg and beat again. Sift together the flour, cocoa powder, baking powder and cinnamon and fold into butter mixture.

Heat the milk then combine with bicarbonate of soda and golden syrup and stir into the cake mixture. Spoon mixture into the tin and bake for 1 hour.

Remove from the oven and cool in the tin for 10 minutes before turning out onto a wire rack to cool completely.

To serve, dust with icing sugar or ice with chocolate frosting, such as Best Ever Icing on page 186, if preferred.

Kathy Mitchell, Varsity Lakes

OMI'S TRADITIONAL ALMOND BUTTERMILK CAKE

My late mum, Heidi, used to make this cake and it became a family favourite over the decades. My parents are of German background and home cooking was a big part of my upbringing. I can recall coming home from school and the aroma of vanilla and roasted almonds wafting from the kitchen as my brother and I raced inside for our afternoon tea.

It is a recipe I still frequently make. It became 'Omi Cake' (German for grandma) for my two (now adult) daughters and we all recall with great love memories of our lovely omi, my mum who died in June of last year. She would have been delighted to see it used as part of a fundraiser for the flood victims.

The best bits are the extra crunchy bits on the edges – yum!

250ml (1 cup) buttermilk
2 eggs, lightly beaten
¾ teaspoon almond extract
210g (1½ cups) plain flour
2 teaspoons baking powder
pinch salt
230g (1 cup) sugar

TOPPING

4 tablespoons butter
145g (⅔ cup) sugar
60g (½ cup) slivered almonds
2 tablespoons double or thickened cream
2 tablespoons plain flour

Preheat oven to 180°C. Grease a 20cm x 30cm lamington tin and line with baking paper.

Whisk buttermilk lightly in a large mixing bowl. Beat in eggs one at a time, then add almond extract. Sift together flour, baking powder and salt and stir with the sugar into the buttermilk mixture.

Pour mixture into tin and bake for 25–30 minutes or until lightly browned and a skewer inserted into the centre of the cake comes out clean. Remove from the oven and leave in the tin to cool.

For the topping, combine all ingredients in a small saucepan and stir over low heat until the butter has melted. Spoon topping mixture over the cake and return to the oven for a further 10–12 minutes. Remove from the oven and allow the cake to cool in the tin.

Note: Cream can be used instead of buttermilk. Whip the cream to soft peaks.

Monica Hailes, Mermaid Waters

ORANGE CAKE

I would make this cake on a regular basis when my family was growing up; it is a favourite with everyone and so easy to make, good for when you have to whip a cake up in a hurry to take somewhere special.

125g (½ cup) butter
grated zest and strained juice of 1 orange
170g (¾ cup) caster sugar
2 eggs, separated
300g (2 cups) self-raising flour
pinch salt
3–4 tablespoons milk

ICING
125g (1 cup) icing sugar
1 tablespoon butter, softened
1 tablespoon orange juice

Preheat oven to 180°C. Lightly grease a loaf tin and line with baking paper.

Cream butter, orange zest and sugar until light and fluffy. Add egg yolks one at a time, beating well after each.

Sift together the flour and salt and fold into butter mixture alternately with orange juice and milk, beginning and ending with flour.

Beat egg whites until stiff peaks form and gently fold into the batter. Pour batter into the tin and bake for 35–40 minutes. Remove the cake from the oven and turn out onto a wire rack to cool completely.

For the icing, sift icing sugar into a small bowl and beat in the butter and orange juice until the mixture is smooth. Spread over cooled cake.

Lyn Mechen, Brassall

ORANGE AND ALMOND CAKE WITH ORANGE SAUCE

2 large navel oranges
6 eggs at room temperature
255g (2½ cups) almond meal
230g (1 cup) caster sugar
1 teaspoon baking powder
2 tablespoons ricotta cheese
50g (⅓ cup) flaked almonds

SAUCE
125g (½ cup) butter
115g (½ cup) caster sugar
2 teaspoons finely grated orange zest
1 tablespoon orange-flavoured liqueur

Place whole oranges in a saucepan, cover with water and boil gently for 30 minutes. Remove the oranges from heat and allow to cool before pureeing in a food processor or with a hand blender. Add the remaining ingredients, except flaked almonds, and process until combined.

Pour batter into tin, top with flaked almonds and bake for 40–50 minutes.

To test if the cake is cooked, insert a wooden skewer into the centre and if it comes out clean then the cake is cooked, but if cake mixture is clinging to the skewer, cook a further 5 minutes.

Remove the cake from the oven and turn onto a wire rack to cool.

For the sauce, combine ingredients in a small saucepan and stir until the butter has melted.

Annie Sims, Brookfield

ORANGE POPPY SEED CAKE

This is the most expected cake at our dinner parties with family and friends. I can make it with my eyes closed.

250g (1 cup) butter
345g (1½ cups) caster sugar
1 tablespoon orange zest
¼ teaspoon vanilla extract
4 eggs
300g (2 cups) plain flour
2½ teaspoons baking powder
¼ teaspoon salt
250ml (1 cup) milk
80g (½ cup) poppy seeds

SYRUP
60ml (¼ cup) orange juice
55g (¼ cup) caster sugar

Preheat oven to 180°C. Grease a 26cm cake tin and line with baking paper.

Cream the butter, sugar, orange zest and vanilla until light and fluffy. Add eggs one at a time, beating well after each. Sift together the flour, baking powder and salt and fold into the butter mixture alternately with the milk. Stir in the poppy seeds and pour mixture into the tin, smoothing the top.

Bake for 50–60 minutes, or until a skewer inserted into the centre of the cake comes out clean.

For the syrup, combine orange juice and sugar in a small saucepan and bring to the boil, stirring to dissolve the sugar.

Remove cake from the oven and prick with a fork. Pour over the hot syrup and leave to cool completely.

Geeta Bhasin, Kenmore

Pecan Nut Cake

An oldie but a goodie. Easy to make, foolproof and keeps well.

300g (2 cups) plain flour
2 teaspoons baking powder
370g (2 cups) brown sugar
125g (½ cup) butter
1 teaspoon bicarbonate of soda
250ml (1 cup) milk
1 egg, lightly beaten
1 teaspoon nutmeg
¼ cup chopped pecans

Preheat oven to 180°C. Grease a 20cm springform tin.

Sift flour and baking powder together, then stir in brown sugar. Rub in the butter until mixture resembles fine breadcrumbs – this can also be done in a food processor.

Spread half of this mixture evenly over the base of the tin.

Dissolve bicarbonate of soda in milk and add beaten egg and nutmeg. Add milk mixture to the reserved flour mixture and stir to combine. Pour over the base mixture in the tin and sprinkle with the pecans.

Bake for 1 hour. Remove from the oven and rest in the tin for 5 minutes before turning out onto a wire rack to cool completely.

Trish Wild, Birkdale

QUICK SPECIAL FRUIT CAKE

150g (1 cup) self-raising flour, sifted
400g tin sweetened condensed milk
375g (3 cups) mixed dried fruit

Preheat oven to 160°C. Grease a 23cm tin and line with baking paper.

Combine all ingredients in a large mixing bowl. Spoon the mixture into the tin and smooth the surface.

Bake for 45 minutes or until a skewer inserted into the centre of the cake comes out clean. Cool in the tin for 10 minutes before turning out onto a wire rack to cool completely.

Note: This recipe can also be made in a slice tin for a quick fruit slice.

Anne Rostedt, Holland Park West

RASPBERRY AND WHITE CHOCOLATE MUFFINS

These are so yummy and easy to make.

300g (2 cups) self-raising flour
165g (¾ cup, firmly packed) brown sugar
1 egg, lightly beaten
185ml (¾ cup) buttermilk
125ml (½ cup) vegetable oil
100g (1 cup) frozen raspberries – do not defrost
170g (1 cup) white chocolate chips

Preheat oven to 190°C. Grease or line a 12-cup muffin tray.

Sift flour into large mixing bowl, add sugar and stir to combine. Whisk together egg, buttermilk and oil in a small bowl and add to the dry ingredients with the raspberries and chocolate chips. Stir the mixture only until it is just combined.

Three-quarter fill each muffin cup and bake for about 15–20 minutes.

Serve muffins dusted with icing sugar.

Janelle Kilgus, Morayfield

STEAMED NUT LOAF

This recipe was given to me by my late Aunty Jean, one of those unrelated aunts who looked after me for a long time, and I loved her dearly. These loaves freeze well.

140g (2 cups) bran cereal
220g (1 cup) sugar
500ml (2 cups) milk
2 tablespoons golden syrup
300g (2 cups) self-raising flour
2 teaspoons bicarbonate of soda
250g (2 cups) dried mixed fruit
185g (1½ cups) chopped walnuts or pecans
1 teaspoon lemon essence

Place bran cereal, sugar, milk and golden syrup in a large mixing bowl and leave to soak, covered, overnight.

Lightly grease 3 nut loaf tins with removable ends.

Add the flour, bicarbonate of soda, mixed fruit, nuts and essence to the soaked mixture and stir well. Place the caps on one end of each tin. Spoon mixture into the tins to half fill them and cover the top with a double layer of foil secured with kitchen string. Using a skewer, pierce a small hole in the foil.

Stand the tins upright in a tall boiler and fill the pan with enough boiling water to come halfway up the tins. Cover the pan and heat until the water is boiling. Reduce the heat to a simmer and cook for 1½ hours.

Remove the tins from the boiler and allow to cool before unmoulding the loaves.

Serve sliced and spread with butter.

Sue Lucas, Ashmore

SULTANA SCONES

I learned this recipe when I was in Scholarship (Year 8) and we used to walk to the local state school (Charleville) from the Catholic school for domestic science around 1959.

300g (2 cups) self-raising flour
1 tablespoon butter, softened
1 tablespoon caster sugar
2 tablespoons sultanas
1 egg, lightly beaten
125ml (½ cup) milk

Preheat oven to 210°C. Lightly grease a baking tray.

Sift flour into a mixing bowl and lightly rub in butter with fingertips. Mix through the sugar and sultanas. Add egg and milk, stirring with the blade of a blunt knife. Turn dough out onto a floured surface and lightly knead.

Press dough out to a thickness of 2cm with a floured hand. Cut with a floured scone cutter and place on the tray approximately 1cm apart, allowing room for expansion.

Bake for 10 minutes. Remove the tray from the oven and slide the scones onto a clean tea towel, fold tea towel over scones and leave to cool.

Serve with butter or whipped cream and strawberry jam.

Note: Wholemeal self-raising flour can be used if preferred.

Claire Jolliffe, Buderim

Walnut Cake

125g (½ cup) butter
170g (¾ cup) caster sugar
1 teaspoon vanilla essence
2 eggs, lightly beaten
300g (2 cups) self-raising flour
pinch salt
1 teaspoon mixed spice
125ml (½ cup) milk
60g (½ cup) chopped walnuts

Icing

125g (1 cup) icing sugar
1 tablespoon butter, softened
1 tablespoon lemon juice

Preheat oven to 180°C. Lightly grease a 23cm ring tin.

Cream butter, sugar and vanilla until light and fluffy. Beat in the eggs one at a time. Sift together the flour, salt and spice and fold into the butter mixture alternately with the milk and chopped nuts, beginning and ending with flour.

Pour batter into tin, smooth the top and bake for 30–35 minutes. Remove from the oven and turn out onto a wire rack to cool completely.

For the icing, sift icing sugar into a small bowl and beat in the butter and lemon juice until the mixture is smooth. Spread the top of the cake with the icing.

Lyn Mechen, Brassall

YOGHURT CAKE

125g (½ cup) butter
690g (3 cups) caster sugar
6 eggs, separated
250g (1 cup) yoghurt
450g (3 cups) plain flour
1 tablespoon baking powder
pinch salt
juice and finely grated zest of 1 lemon

Preheat the oven to 180°C. Grease a 25cm or large fluted cake tin and line with baking paper.

Cream the butter and sugar until light and fluffy then add egg yolks and yoghurt.

Sift together the flour, baking powder and salt and fold into the butter mixture with the lemon juice and zest.

In a separate bowl, beat the egg whites until stiff peaks form then fold into the creamed mixture and pour into the tin.

Bake for 1 hour. Remove from the oven and rest in the tin for 20 minutes before turning out onto a wire rack to cool completely.

Serve cake dusted with icing sugar.

Barbara Tahan, Albany Creek

BEST EVER ICING FOR CAKES AND CUPCAKES

250g (1 cup) softened butter
125ml (½ cup) milk
1kg (8 cups) icing sugar

Place all ingredients in large bowl and mix well until combined and fluffy.

Icing may be coloured with food colouring as desired, and flavoured with 1 tablespoon vanilla extract. For chocolate icing, beat in 60 g (½ cup) cocoa. Orange, raspberry or strawberry essences can also be used to flavour icing.

Tip: Any icing not used can be stored in airtight container in fridge for up to a month, or frozen for up to 3 months.

Maggie Littlefair, Camp Hill

PRESERVES

FRAN'S CHILLI JAM

This is a dear friend's recipe for chilli jam. It is sensational and tastes great on sandwiches and BLTs, and with lamb and cheese. I am frequently asked for this recipe. You will never eat the stuff out of a bottle again, unless you are my son!

775g (5 cups) finely chopped red capsicum
660g (3 cups) sugar
3 cloves garlic, very finely chopped
5–6 long red chillies, finely chopped
750ml (3 cups) vinegar

Put all ingredients in a large, heavy-based pot and stir to combine. Bring to the boil then reduce heat to a simmer and cook for 2 hours or until the mixture has a jam-like consistency.

Remove from heat and pour into sterilised jars and seal.

Store in the refrigerator.

Note: If preferred, the capsicum can be chopped in a food processor. To increase the heat, use small bird's eye chillies.

Jenny Woodward, ABC TV weather presenter

LEMON CURD

This is a prizewinning recipe! In the 1999 EKKA, the lemon curd came second, and in 2000 the passionfruit curd came first. What the judges didn't know is that the first place passionfruit was the first time I had ever made that flavour! It gave me a smile.

Both recipes are school fete favourites. These curds are a real 'comfort food' – they are sensational on morning toast, crumpets or scones, or as a filling in pre-baked tarts. I have held the recipe tightly – but this cookbook is the best reason to share. Enjoy!

4 eggs
150ml (⅔ cup) lemon juice
65g (¼ cup) unsalted butter
325g (1½ cups) sugar

Lightly beat eggs in a large heatproof bowl and put aside.

Place lemon juice, butter and sugar in a small saucepan and stir over low heat until the sugar and butter have melted. Very slowly pour hot lemon mixture over eggs, stirring constantly.

Transfer the whole mixture back to the saucepan and cook on very low heat, continually stirring, ensuring it does not boil. Remove as soon as the mixture thickens, pour into sterilised glass jars, seal and allow to cool.

Store in the refrigerator.

Passionfruit Curd: Using exactly the same proportions, substitute passionfruit for lemon. Strain all the passionfruit juice, retaining the pips from only 1 or 2 passionfruit so that it is not mistaken for lemon. If the juice is exceptionally sweet, then add 20–30ml lemon juice to the mixture.

Monica Raferty, Red Hill

MARGE'S EASY PICKLES

This recipe was given to me by an elderly lady to try. Not being a pickle lover, I was converted and will not buy shop pickles after tasting these. It is very easy to make.

1kg onions, thinly sliced
2 tablespoons salt
225g (¾ cup) sugar
¾ teaspoon curry powder
1 teaspoon turmeric
1 dessertspoon mustard powder
500ml (2 cups) vinegar
480g tin crushed pineapple
2 tablespoons cornflour
2 tablespoons water

Sprinkle thinly sliced onions with salt and leave covered overnight.

Drain the onions and place in a large saucepan with sugar, curry powder, turmeric, mustard powder and vinegar. Slowly bring to the boil, reduce heat to a simmer and cook, covered, for 15 minutes. Add pineapple and simmer for a further 15 minutes.

Mix together the cornflour and water in a small bowl and add to the pickle mixture.

Stir until thickened, then remove from the heat and pour into sterilised bottles.

Seal and allow to cool before storing in a dark, cool and dry place.

Marlene Goodman, Warana

Tomato Pickles

2kg tomatoes, chopped
2kg onion, chopped
½ tablespoon curry powder
½ tablespoon dry mustard
1 tablespoon salt
1 teaspoon turmeric
180ml (¾ cup) white or brown vinegar
2 tablespoons cornflour
60ml (¼ cup) water

Place all ingredients except the cornflour and water in a large saucepan. Stir to combine then bring to the boil. Reduce the heat and simmer for 20 minutes or until vegetables are very soft.

Mix cornflour and water and add a little at a time to the tomato mixture, stirring until it has thickened. Remove from the heat and pour into sterilised bottles, seal and allow to cool.

Note: Other vegetables such as cauliflower or beans can be used.

Gail Davis, Linville

INDEX